*Robert Hayden*

Twayne's United States Authors Series

Warren French, Editor
*Indiana University, Indianapolis*

TUSAS 471

ROBERT HAYDEN
(1913–1980)
*Photograph courtesy of*
*Mrs. Erma Hayden*

# Robert Hayden

By Fred M. Fetrow
*United States Naval Academy*

*Twayne Publishers • Boston*

*To my wife, Miriam
and my children, Blake and Valry*

*Robert Hayden*

Fred M. Fetrow

Copyright © 1984 by G. K. Hall & Company
All Rights Reserved
Published by Twayne Publishers
A Division of G. K. Hall & Company
70 Lincoln Street
Boston, Massachusetts 02111

Book Production by John Amburg
Book Design by Barbara Anderson

Printed on permanent / durable acid-free
paper and bound in the United States of
America.

**Library of Congress Cataloging in Publication Data**

Fetrow, Fred M.
  Robert Hayden.

  (Twayne's United States authors series; TUSAS 471)
  Bibliography: p. 151
  Includes index.
  1. Hayden, Robert Earl—Criticism and interpretation.
I. Title.   II. Series.
PS3515.A9363Z66   1984      811'.52      83–26581
ISBN 0–8057–7412–2

# Contents

# About the Author

Fred M. Fetrow, a native of O'Neill, Nebraska, is an associate professor of English at the United States Naval Academy in Annapolis, Maryland. During his tenure on the faculty, which commenced in 1974, he has served as director of freshman English and as chairman of the Department of English. He received the Ph.D. from the University of Nebraska, specializing in Restoration–Eighteenth Century British literature. Professor Fetrow is the author of several scholarly articles ranging from Renaissance drama and poetry to contemporary American fiction, and including five articles on the life and poetry of Robert Hayden.

# Preface

Robert Hayden (1913–1980) lived and wrote poetry during a turbulent period in American history. His private life had its own turbulence, apart from, and yet reflective of, that larger cultural upheaval. Because he captured in his poetic art both the public event and private nuance (and the linkages among them) of twentieth-century American life, his poetry stands as a relevant record of its time, as well as a sustained exhibition of artistic achievement. Yet Hayden's poetic career also traces a long record of neglect and rejection. He refused the entrapment of limitation, whether the snare took the form of second-class citizenship in a "literary ghetto" offered sporadically to black poets since the Harlem Renaissance by the white literary establishment, or whether the trap was set in the 1960s by black militantism with the bait of the black aesthetic. This refusal cost him dearly in those quarters that could extract the prices of critical neglect, public anonymity, and racial rejection. Yet it also afforded him the sometimes painful possibility to fulfill his artistic destiny in true faith to his art and his transcendent humanity.

That ascent to fulfillment left behind a canon of poetry imbued with intense feeling, crafted with meticulous skill, and illuminative of universal human experience. It deserves our attention, and we need its humanizing effect. This volume, the first full-length study of Robert Hayden, provides preliminary information about his life and attempts to do some small justice to the wonder of his work. The chapters have been arranged to present first a biographical and literary survey of its subject, and then to provide critical analysis of his poetry. The analytical chapters have been ordered in the chronological sequence of Hayden's major publications and organized to treat the poems according to subject categories, thematic concerns, and poetic techniques. This progression is designed to trace and thus clarify the poet's evolution into a major voice in modern American literature. The purpose of this study then is to assist readers, students, scholars, and critics in becoming more familiar with, and more knowledgeable about, Robert Hayden's life and poetry. Of course the implicit aim of the book has its basis in the sharing of such knowledge; those who knew Robert Hayden and read his work inevitably agree that his words about another lover of truth readily apply to the poet who wrote them:

> this man, superb in love and logic, this man
> shall be remembered.

Fred M. Fetrow

*United States Naval Academy*

# Acknowledgments

For a grant to begin this study, I am indebted to the United States Naval Academy Research Council. My thanks to William T. Woolwine for his early encouragement of my interest in Robert Hayden, and to Clarence "Soc" Glasrud for helping me find a feasible outlet for that interest. Mrs. Helen Branham and the rest of the staff of the Nimitz Library at the Naval Academy have been most helpful. Besides typing the manuscript, Mrs. Barbara Rutledge and Ms. Deborah Queen provided valuable editorial assistance and invaluable moral support. Special gratitude goes to Michael S. Harper; his encouragement and the subtle pressure of his implicit expectations have made all the difference.

Finally, I wish to thank the three people without whom the book would never have reached completion: my wife, Miriam, deserves the most thanks for the least tangible contribution—who else would tolerate being read aloud to night after night? Mrs. Erma Hayden has corrected my errors in fact, guided my progress, and given her kind approbation along the way. My debt to Robert Hayden can never be repaid. He made himself available to my questions, answered them in ways I could understand, provided me with poems in manuscript and materials unavailable anywhere else, and took as much interest in my work as I had in his. Throughout it all, he kept writing those wonderful poems that made the writing about them truly a labor of love.

For permission to quote from copyrighted material, acknowledgment is made to the following:

Mrs. Erma Hayden for *Heart-Shape in the Dust* (1940), *The Lion and the Archer* (1948), and *Figure of Time* (1955).
W. W. Norton & Co. for *Angle of Ascent* (1975) and *American Journal* (1982) and Effendi Press for *American Journal* (1978).

# Chronology

1913    Robert Hayden (born Asa Bundy Sheffey) born on August 4 in Detroit, Michigan. Reared by foster parents, William and Sue Ellen Hayden, in "Paradise Valley" area, St. Antoine Street.

1918–1930    Educated in Detroit public schools; placed in the "sight conservation" class because of extremely poor vision. Studied violin for several years at the Detroit Institute of Musical Art. Wrote stories, plays, and poems as early as grammar school; "discovers" Dunbar, Millay, Cullen, et al. as young man (ca. age 16).

1931    Publishes first poem, "Africa" (an imitation of Cullen's "Heritage"), in *Abbot's Monthly.*

1932–1936    Attended Detroit City College (now Wayne State University).

1936–1940    Worked as writer and researcher on the WPA Federal Writers' Project, Detroit. Publishes "Autumnal" in *American Stuff* (1937). Enrolled as part-time student at University of Michigan, Ann Arbor. Won Hopwood Minor Award for poetry, University of Michigan, summer (1938).

1940    Married Erma Inez Morris, pianist and teacher in the Detroit public schools (June 15). Worked on the Federal Historical Records Survey. Wrote music and drama criticism for the *Michigan Chronicle*. First book of poems, *Heart-shape in the Dust*, published by Louis O. Martin's Falcon Press, Detroit.

1941    Moved to Ann Arbor to complete education at the University of Michigan; studied under the poet W. H. Auden. Prepares manuscript of "The Black Spear" for Hopwood competition. Group of poems published in *The Negro Caravan*, Dryden Press, New York.

1942     Became a member of the Baha'i World Faith together with wife. Daughter Maia born (October 5). Won Hopwood Major Award for Poetry. Received Bachelor of Arts degree from Wayne State University.

1944     Received Master of Arts degree in English from University of Michigan. Elected to Phi Kappa Phi. Appointed teaching assistant in English at the University.

1946     "Middle Passage" published in Edwin Seaver's *Cross Section*, Fischer, New York. Appointed Assistant Professor of English, Fisk University, Nashville, Tennessee.

1947     Awarded Rosenwald Fellowship in Creative Writing. "Frederick Douglass" published in the *Atlantic Monthly* (February issue).

1948     *The Lion and the Archer: Poems*, published in collaboration with Myron O'Higgins and illustrated by William Demby. Launched the Counterpoise Series organized by Hayden and a small group of writers and artists at Fisk.

1950     On leave of absence from Fisk, moved with his family to New York in order that his daughter might begin her education in an unsegregated school. Wrote while his wife taught music and creative movement at Little Red Schoolhouse. Several poems appeared in the Hughes-Bontemps anthology *Poetry of the Negro*, Doubleday, New York.

1951     Returned with his family to Nashville.

1954     Received Ford Foundation grant for travel and writing in Mexico. Promoted to associate professor at Fisk.

1955     Published *Figure of Time: Poems*, in the Counterpoise Series, with illustrations by Aaron Douglas and Yvonne Cole, Hemphill Press, Nashville.

1955–1960     Poems translated into Serbian, Japanese, Spanish, Italian, Russian, and German; also broadcast by the British Broadcasting Company.

1962     Poems appeared in Rosey Pool's anthology *Beyond the Blues*, London. *A Ballad of Remembrance*, second book of poems, published in London, initial volume in Paul Breman's Heritage Series.

1966   Awarded Grand Prize for Poetry for *A Ballad of Remembrance* at First World Festival of Negro Arts in Dakar, Senegal. *Selected Poems* published by October House, New York. Poems featured in *A Hand Is on the Gate*, which ran at the Longacre Theater in New York for several months.

1967   Poet-in-residence at Indiana State University during the summer term. Edited *Kaleidoscope: Poems by American Negro Poets*, Harcourt Brace World, New York. Poems recorded for *Today's Poets*, issued by Scholastic Folkways. Appointed Poetry Editor of *World Order*, quarterly journal of the Baha'i Faith. Promoted to Professor of English at Fisk.

1968   Visiting Professor of English, University of Michigan. Invited to read with Derek Walcott at the Library of Congress. Poems recorded for the Library of Congress Archives. Appeared with Walcott in TV poetry film, "Middle Passage and Beyond," made at WETA, Washington, D.C.

1969   Received Mayor's Bronze Medal for distinguished achievement by a native Detroiter from Mayor Jerome Cavanaugh, in January, at a banquet sponsored by Cultural Committee of Second Baptist Church. Bingham Professor at University of Louisville (spring semester). Resigned from Fisk University. Visiting Poet at the University of Washington, Seattle (summer semester). Appointed in fall to University of Michigan as professor of English.

1970   *Words in the Mourning Time* published by October House, New York. National Book Award nominee. Received Russell Loines Award for Distinguished poetic achievement from National Institute of Arts and Letters. At work on "The Night-Blooming Cereus." Began association with Scott, Foresman & Company, Glenview, Illinois, as writer, consultant, and editor. Poems in their record album *Some Haystacks Don't Even Have Any Needle*.

1971   Read "The Night-Blooming Cereus" as the Phi Beta Kappa poem at the University of Michigan. Coeditor, *Afro-American Literature: An Introduction*, Harcourt

Brace Jovanovich, New York. *Spectrum in Black*, album of recordings, published by Scott, Foresman & Company, Glenview.

1972   *The Night-Blooming Cereus*, collection of poems, published in London by Paul Breman, to mark tenth anniversary of his Heritage Series. On poetry staff at the Breadloaf Writers' Conference, Middlebury College, Vermont (August). Coauthor, *How I write/1*, Harcourt Brace Jovanovich. Editor, modern American poetry section, *The United States in Literature*, Scott, Foresman & Company.

1973   *Interviews with Black Writers* with John O'Brien, Liveright, New York.

1974   Visiting poet, Connecticut College (spring semester). At work on "Angle of Ascent." "In Memoriam Malcolm X," musical allegory by composer T. J. Anderson with text by Hayden, sung by Betty Allen, given first performance in Avery Fisher Hall, New York (April).

1975   *Angle of Ascent: New and Selected Poems* published by Liveright, New York. Received honorary degree of Doctor of Letters, Grand Valley State College, Michigan. Elected fellow of the Academy of American Poets with a stipend of $10,000. Appointed Consultant in Poetry to the Library of Congress.

1976   Commission received from Founders Society, Detroit Institute of Arts, for poem on John Brown to be included in a portfolio of screenprints after the *John Brown* series by Jacob Lawrence. Second invitation to write Phi Beta Kappa poem for the Michigan Chapter. Read "American Journal" (March). Received honorary degree of Doctor of Letters from Brown University (June). Assumed duties as Consultant in Poetry to the Library of Congress (September).

1977   Reappointed Consultant in Poetry to the Library of Congress. Participated in Inauguration Series of Poetry Readings, Folger Shakespeare Library, Washington, D.C. (January). Received 1977 Art Award from Michigan Foundation for the Arts (April). Received honorary degree of Doctor of Letters from Benedict College, Columbia, South Carolina (May). Received honorary degree of Doctor of Letters from Wayne State University (June).

1978    *American Journal* published by Effendi Press, Taunton, Massachusetts (May). "John Brown" published by Founders Society, Detroit Institute of Arts, in portfolio, *The Legend of John Brown*, with screenprints by Jacob Lawrence.

1979    Inducted into the Academy of American Poets and Institute of Arts and Letters (May). In New York to attend annual meeting of the Academy of American Poets and to deliver manuscript of latest collection of poems to editors at Liveright Press (December).

1980    Read "The Night-Blooming Cereus" at "A White House Salute to American Poetry," a reception for prominent American poets (January). "A Tribute to Robert Hayden," sponsored by the Center for Afro-American and African Studies, in collaboration with the Eva Jessye Afro-American Music Collection, University of Michigan, Ann Arbor (February 24). Died of respiratory embolism at age sixty-six. Buried in Fairview Cemetery in Ann Arbor, Michigan (February 25).

1982    *American Journal*, collection of Hayden's last poems, posthumously published by Liveright Press.

# Chapter One
# Living Is the Thing
## Paradise Valley

Robert Hayden's birth on August 4, 1913, on Beacon Street in the Detroit black ghetto later known ironically as "Paradise Valley," was as obscure as his subsequent poetic career was for so long largely unheralded. The circumstances of his early life have their own drama, laced with the same sort of cosmic irony that pervades much of Hayden's mature poetry. The poet's effort to transcend and yet subsume his background significantly influenced and informed his artistic endeavor, so a sketch of Hayden's early years can be illuminating as a preface to the sustained study of his poetry.[1]

Robert Hayden was born of the rather fragile union of Asa Sheffey and Ruth Finn. The couple named their infant "Asa Bundy" for his father, and the doctor who delivered him. Hayden's parents were young, impoverished blacks living on the raw edge of desperation in a blatantly racist urban society, and, at least partially due to these circumstances, the poet's early life took an almost bizarre turn. His father either could not or would not provide financial support or domestic stability; like a Tennessee Williams character, Asa Sheffey "fell in love with long distance," leaving the responsibility of raising the baby to Hayden's mother. She, in turn, out of financial need and personal aspirations for a stage career, soon also departed, to seek employment in Buffalo, New York, leaving the baby with her neighbors, William and Sue Ellen Hayden. What she thought would be a temporary separation turned out to be permanent. The Haydens took young Asa into their home and eventually into their hearts, and raised him as their own. They renamed the child Robert Earl Hayden, and from that moment, in effect, both Asa Sheffeys "disappeared." His natural parents eventually divorced, and both later remarried, but Robert remained a "Hayden" all his life.

Indeed, Robert Hayden grew up, married, had a family, and reached middle age in the belief that his foster parents had adopted him when he was of preschool age. He was dismayed to discover

1

when he was forty years old that in fact William and Sue Hayden had never accomplished that legal formality; that legally, he was still Asa Sheffey. This revelation came about in 1953 as Hayden sent to Lansing, Michigan, for his birth certificate under the name of Robert Hayden, in order to obtain a passport. There was no record; he did not exist as Robert Hayden. Since Asa Sheffey existed only as a name on a birth certificate, and since his foster parents were both dead by then, Robert's natural mother had to file an affidavit establishing that in fact Robert Earl Hayden and Asa Bundy Sheffey were one and the same.[2] Although Hayden subconsciously strove to resolve this quite literal identity crisis for most of his adult life, only finally in 1978 did he legally "change" his name to Robert Hayden.

In addition to a displacement of identity as a child, young Robert's maturing years were marked by psychic assault and physical disability. Although the Haydens provided true parental concern and real love, along with a strong dose of old-fashioned, guilt-inducing, hell-and-damnation religion, his foster mother often reminded him of her charity, his ingratitude, and his natural mother's unworthiness. As a youngster, Robert occasionally was allowed to visit his mother in Buffalo, and Ruth Sheffey returned periodically to Paradise Valley to see her son. When Robert was a teenager, she returned to Detroit to stay, and moved in with the Haydens, increasing the "family" to include Robert, his foster parents, his natural mother, and "Aunt Roxie," the daughter of his foster mother by a previous marriage. Although Hayden's natural mother eventually left the house, she continued living next door to the Haydens.

The proximity of emotionally competitive parent figures produced divisions of love, loyalty, and resentment that took an enormous psychological toll on the boy as he tried to cope with the "chronic angers" of that household. Of those diverse permutations of "divide and antagonize," Hayden recalled mainly the conflicts between foster and natural mother for his affection, and the "ganging up" of the three women against the quietly enduring and often unappreciated father figure in an essentially matriarchal "minisociety." Robert, out of the simple immaturity of youth and a kind of emotional necessity, frequently found himself taking sides in these quarrels. The changeability of his allegiances contrasted with the nagging regularity of the emotional distress he experienced in those days. Even in his advanced years, Hayden recalled his youth with ambivalence, finding comfort in memories of shared love, yet almost visibly flinching in remembered response to the psychic trauma of his "unusual" family life.

If that was not enough, Robert suffered from an early age from extreme myopia. His nearsightedness was so severe that it denied him the physical activity and participation in sports one ordinarily associates with teenaged boys. However, in retrospect, the handicap probably fostered his predilection for the arts in general and poetry in particular. He seemed to compensate for the limitation by developing a remarkable sensitivity to visual and auditory stimulation. He loved music, for example, and through financial sacrifice by his family, he took up the violin, for several years taking lessons at the Detroit Institute of Musical Art. He played in the Sunday School orchestra, and in the grammar- and high-school programs during those years, but finally gave up the violin when he could no longer read the music without putting his nose in the charts. His activity as a musical performer was relatively shortlived, but Hayden retained his love of music throughout his life, and his poetry reflects both his knowledge of and his sensitivity to rhythm and tonal effects. In a comparably similar pattern of progression, Hayden's childhood love of colors and coloring books ultimately gave way to the mature adult's penchant for papers, notebooks, and stationeries. His interest in and love of poetic possibilities among tactile, auditory, and chromatic experiences never diminished. Hayden's eyes failed him, yet perhaps also "saved" him for something more important.

Reading provided young Hayden with refuge, resource, and, ultimately, with reward. Although his vision was so limited that by high-school age he was placed in "sight conservation" classes within the Detroit public-school system, the young myopic as early as grammar school sought escape from domestic turmoil and the ghetto grind in imaginative literature of diverse quality and genre. Not content with a passive form of escapism, he wrote in imitation of the movies he had seen, composing amateurish stories and plays. He discovered new worlds in the Detroit Public Library, and as he moved vicariously into those worlds, he intensified his efforts to create his own. Poetry naturally appealed to him. The genre, which said the most in the fewest words, demanded the least of his physical vision yet provided his acute sensibility a vision of perceived beauty not readily apparent in his "real" world. Later he began to write poems of his own, as he read voraciously the poetry of others, discovering in high school Paul Laurence Dunbar, Countee Cullen, Carl Sandburg, and Edna St. Vincent Millay, among others, in his search for a "reality" more tolerable than his own.

Influenced by his reading, Hayden continued to write poetry throughout his high-school years, and he was by age sixteen consciously an aspiring poet. He certainly thought of himself in those terms when the first publication of his youthful effort came shortly after his graduation from high school in 1930. Not surprisingly, "Africa," a derivative imitation of Countee Cullen's "Heritage" (1925), showed more hope than promise when it appeared in the July issue of *Abbot's Monthly* in 1931. Written in five eight-line stanzas of four couplets each, "Africa" confounds sincere emotional intensity with artificially stylized, archaic poetic diction. At best the poem is magazine verse appropriate to its context. Nevertheless, it exhibits the positive influences of Hayden's reading, and the seriousness of his intentions; it is a very early poem of a young poet who has yet to find his own voice. Hayden wrote "Africa" and other essentially imitative poems during an "interim" period when the poet coupled his rather romantic notions about artistic agony and soul-searing struggle with the harsh reality of a Depression-era young black who survived with odd jobs and naive hope, as he tried to write poetry and find a way to finance more formal education. He filled his days methodically if not obsessively with his own informal program of education in contemporary poetry:

I certainly was more devoted to poetry than to anything else. I cared more for it than I did for anything else. I was always reading poetry, always trying to write it. I had a friend at the public library, Marie Alice Hanson, to whom I dedicated in part my latest book *Words in the Mourning Time.* Marie Alice would put the new books of poetry aside for me, and when I kept them out beyond the due date she would sometimes pay the fines. She encouraged my love for poetry.[3]

I remember going through the library and getting the volume edited by Alain Locke called *The New Negro.* I discovered those poets and I went to the library and got individual volumes by each of them. . . . At that time I'd go to the library and get out all the anthologies, and I just knew everybody almost.[4]

## Colleged

The year of his first published poem marks another milestone in Robert Hayden's career. In later years he readily acknowledged and even "catalogued" those who made it possible for him to continue his education by enrolling in Wayne City College (later Wayne State University) in 1931: the social-services caseworker assigned to the Haydens during one of the periods when the family was forced onto the welfare rolls, who encouraged Robert and helped him get a scholarship and admission to college; "Pa" Hayden, the coal-wagon driver committed to his son's education, who sacrificed to help Robert attend school in the summers of his teenage years; Aunt Roxie and the elder neighbors who dropped quarters into his palm and took pride in his ambition to get "colleged."

The young man from the Detroit slums approached the college experience with that same seemingly incompatible combination of pragmatic determination and naive idealism. While he took a "practical" major as a means of equipping himself with what he expected would be a marketable skill, he devoted most of his time and energy to decidedly impractical interests in drama and poetry. Although Hayden majored in Spanish, he pursued his interest in poetry, continuing his reading of contemporary American poets, both the first-rate and the merely fashionable, and adding to his own unpublished poems. Many of these he later suggested were almost inevitably imitative of the poets and techniques he encountered in his reading. As an undergraduate, he also exercised "a flair for the dramatic" by participating in college and local drama productions. As he phrased it, "I was stage-struck as a young person, acted all over the place."[5] A few years later, he wrote scripts for both stage and radio, took roles in several plays, and even had some serious aspirations for a dramatic career. Hayden traced these activities to his "genes," citing his natural mother's stage presence and her sporadic work in legitimate theater and musicals.[6] This "flair" is readily evident in Hayden's subsequent work, which literally abounds in the dramatic elements of situational irony, dialogue, soliloquy, or dramatic monologue. Indeed, several of his mature poems are plays in miniature, complete with plot, characterization, dialogue, and a resultant dramatic intensity.

One of the poet's most vivid memories of his college days in

Detroit contrasts ironically the encouragement he received from
"uneducated" family, friends, and neighbors with a painfully dis-
appointing "educated" response to his poetic endeavors and
hopes. In interviews Hayden frequently told the anecdote about
how his English teacher at Detroit City College, after reading some
of Robert's work, told the young man to forget his foolish dream,
that he simply had no talent, that he should give it up. Hayden
soon came to appreciate an element of justice in the teacher's low
opinion of those early poems, but he never forgot that "discour-
aging word." The recollection provided him special gratification in
returning to his alma mater some twenty-five years later to read his
poetry to an appreciative audience. More importantly, the psychologically traumatic incident contributed to the formulation of a
compassionate teacher and a sensitive poet. As a teacher Hayden
vowed never to treat his student poets so harshly; as a poet he "co-
opted" harsh criticism by becoming his own most severe critic, one
whose work progressed slowly but improved vastly according to the
continuous application of his own exacting standards.

Robert Hayden left Detroit City College in 1936, and, in the
midst of the Great Depression, "graduated" to the Federal
Writers' Project of the Works Progress Administration. He was
assigned to research local history and "Negro folklore," working
specifically on the Underground Railroad in Michigan and the anti-
slavery movement in that area during the abolition era prior to the
Civil War. During the next two years, as a member of the Writers'
Project, he encountered a history of his people previously little
known to him. The research not only enhanced his racial awareness
and pride, but provided him with a wealth of material and knowledge that he would later combine with the "folk knowledge" inherent in his own upbringing in Paradise Valley, an amalgam that
he would ultimately reconstitute artistically in the poetic forms and
subjects for which he is now perhaps most noted.

His membership in the Writer's Project also provided an early
outlet for some of his current work. For example, "Autumnal" appeared in print as part of the Project anthology *American Stuff* in
1937. This poem, a contemplation of death, cast in starkly contrasting images of beauty and horror, appears in pretty good company. *American Stuff* includes poems, short fiction, and essays by
such contemporaries as Richard Wright ("The Ethics of Living Jim
Crow—An Autobiographical Sketch"), Claude McKay (a poem,

"Song of the Moon"), Sterling Brown (a poem, "All Are Gay"),
and Kenneth Rexforth (a poem, "Excerpts from 'The Apple Garths
of Avalon' "). Hayden's "Autumnal" is accompanied by a brief
note on its contributor that suggests that his first book of poems, to
be titled *Flying Shadow*, was scheduled for publication in the fall of
1937. That volume, however, never appeared, and one must sur-
mise that at least some of the poems that would have made up its
content were published in 1940 as part of *Heart-Shape in the Dust*,
Hayden's first published collection.

## The People's Poet

Even as Hayden's employment with the Writers' Project made
him more conscious of his heritage, during this same period he
began to develop the social consciousness so prevalent in the late
1930s among his generation of college-age youth, both white and
black. Inspired by the contemporary activist poets he studied in
school, and influenced by those black writers he read on his own, he
began to write poems "for his people," protesting social conditions
and pleading for social and economic equality. His yearning for an
audience coincided happily with the local political atmosphere of
the times; he was invited to read his essentially polemical verse at
union rallies in support of labor organizing movements in Detroit.
Hayden found immediate and heady acceptance in this role, and
was on one occasion proclaimed "The People's Poet" of Detroit.[7]

The mature poet recalled this period in his career with something
akin to self-conscious amusement, contending that his heart was
then in the right place, but that the heartfelt utterings of an
apprentice poet were probably more propagandistic than artistic. In
retrospect, and in the interest of a valid perspective on the entire
career of Robert Hayden, one can generalize that his initial impulse
to be a public spokesman on behalf of his race was never abandoned. He continued for the ensuing forty years to be a strong
moral voice of his people, even as he matured to become the artist
whose faithfulness to his art subsumed his urge for utilitarian
polemic, even as he vowed publicly and courageously in the militant
1960s, and until his death, that his poetry should not and would not
be limited to "racial utterance." Hayden's development as a poet,

in a sense, can be traced along that line from an early voice limited
to a narrow racial perspective to a spokesman of transcendent
concern for universally human themes, but it is an unbroken line
that begins and ends with his personal, racial, and historical
heritage. Hayden never forgot that heritage, never overlooked that
continuity, and those who wish to grasp the full meaning of his
poetic response to life should not either.

## The 'Prentice Years

''The People's Poet'' returned to academe as a part-time student
at the University of Michigan in 1938. This time he mustered
enough confidence to commit himself fully to his first love; he
enrolled as an English major and finally took up formal study of the
art he had been practicing for over ten years. His devotion was soon
rewarded, as he won in August 1938 the Jule and Avery Hopwood
Award given by the university for his sheaf of poems that grew out
of the reading, study, and writing of the previous decade.[8]
    The manuscript, entitled ''Heart-Shape in the Dust,'' a phrasing
from one of Hayden's favorite Elinor Wylie poems, contains eleven
poems that exhibit both the pitfalls of ''student poetry'' and the
promise of the mature poet to be. The poems range in subject matter from perhaps too many abstract expressions of youthful angst, to
a love sonnet, to some ''heritage'' poems dedicated to the past suffering of his race. The best of these '' 'prentice pieces'' evidence the
young poet's innate acuity of observation, which results frequently
in objective reproduction of sensuous imagery. The collection contains a few precursive hints of the subtle psychological portraiture
that Hayden would produce as his art evolved from emotional assertion to objectively subtle expression based more on connotative and
often ironic implication. One finds few ''pearls'' in this slim
manuscript, but some poems, such as ''Old Woman with Violets''
especially, suggest the gemlike quality with which Hayden would
imbue his later work.
    The love poem, like the manuscript itself, Hayden dedicated to
Erma Inez Morris, a pianist and teacher in the Detroit public
schools. Erma was also reared by ''foster'' parents, an aunt and
uncle, since her parents had divorced, and her mother had died
when Erma was still young. Otherwise, Robert and Erma came from

relatively disparate backgrounds, in that she was of West Indian ancestry and came from West Detroit, at that time a bastion of middle-class black respectability—quite in contrast with Robert's slum upbringing in the lower East Side's Paradise Valley. Hers was an educated and education-oriented family with degrees from Howard University and other good eastern schools; he was the first ever from his family even to attend college. The two young people, however, shared an affinity for the arts and an admiration for each other, and together they nurtured each other's respective aspirations: hers to become a composer and concert pianist; his to become *the* poet of his age.[9]

During their courtship Robert pursued a hectic pace of study, employment, and creative activity. He worked part-time as a music, movie, and drama critic, writing a column called "Stage Door" for the *Michigan Chronicle*, a weekly black newspaper published in Detroit.[10] His other writing coincided in subject matter, if not content, with his newspaper writing. In addition to acting in plays at every opportunity, Hayden wrote scripts for radio-broadcast dramatization and for the local drama groups with which he was associated. One script, entitled "Go Down, Moses," was produced locally, and although according to Hayden it is best forgotten, the subject indicates his interest in historical themes generated by the Writers' Project experience. The play, which was performed probably only two or three times, chronicles the life of Harriet Tubman and her work with the Underground Railroad.[11] As reported in later interviews, Hayden's acting "career" was shortlived and frustrated by too many instances of his trying unsuccessfully to fulfill racial stereotypes in casting and dialogue.

However, these drama activities indirectly reinforced his poetic aspirations. For one thing, the practice in writing dramatic dialogue no doubt had the effect of sharpening his already sensitive ear to cadence, tone, and vocal inference. As an actor, he had the opportunity to meet with an eminently successful contemporary black poet when in the late 1930s Langston Hughes came to Detroit to see a production of one of his many plays. Hayden was in the Hughes play, and thereby managed to meet with the playwright, whose response to Robert's poems was somewhat lukewarm. Hughes, however, tempered Robert's disappointment by encouraging the young man to find his own voice, to keep looking for his individualized perspective.[12]

Through all of these occupational and avocational activities

Hayden's interest in and effort at his poetry never lagged. His editor at the *Michigan Chronicle*, Louis O. Martin, became interested in Robert's work. He decided that the poems of his young columnist deserved a wider audience, and he proposed to start his own press in order to reach it. Hayden, encouraged by Martin's faith in him, worked feverishly to assemble, revise, and enlarge his collection. Louis Martin established the Falcon Press and published Hayden's work as *Heart-Shape in the Dust* in 1940. By the time the book came out, Hayden had left the Writers' Project and had gone on to work on the Federal Historical Records Survey, but as the WPA projects wound down he was soon facing unemployment again, except for the limited income he got for his columns in the *Michigan Chronicle*.

*Heart-Shape* never alleviated this financial distress, but it sold quite well for a time in Detroit, and was even reviewed briefly in the *New York Herald Tribune*. The collection itself now has more than antiquarian interest; it demonstrates Hayden's artistic status at that time, and thus partially reveals how far he came later in his career. The dominant subjects, themes, and techniques indicate much about Hayden's growth as a poet, either through the embedded assets of proclivities in need only of refinement or through the presence of topics or methods to which he seldom or never returned again.

The book contains some forty-seven poems, thirteen of which had formed the content of the 1938 Hopwood Award manuscript bearing the same title. Like that earlier collection, this *Heart-Shape* was dedicated to Erma, here simply but significantly identified as "the source." One can discern the influences of other poets in a number of the poems, and certainly no one would claim that all the works rank consistently high in artistic achievement, but as a whole the collection seems more worthy of praise than the author himself ever admitted. Quite expectedly, the poems frequently show the pervasive influence of the Harlem Renaissance and its more prominent luminaries. For example, one can readily see the inspiration of Langston Hughes in Hayden's lengthy "These Are My People," but whether judged as an elaboration of Hughes's "I, Too, Sing America" or as imitative of his "Let America Be America Again" Hayden's version of the plea for equality and brotherhood is both collective and individualized in its perspective. The eight-page length itself allowed Hayden the space to try his wings, to develop the varied narrative voices so characteristic of later, more refined work. The "trial flight" (as Hayden retrospectively labeled *Heart-Shape*) in such "dialect" poems as "Shine, Mister?," "Bacchanale," and "Ole Jim Crow" captures quite convincingly the speech patterns and concerns of oppressed blacks and fellow ghetto-dwellers, thereby evoking through the indirection of a persona the physical and psychological settings for these "contemporary" pieces. In an historical mode, Hayden uses a dialogue format to sustain the visionary premise of "Gabriel," a tribute to Gabriel Prosser, hanged in 1800 for attempting to lead a slave revolt. The narrator queries Gabriel about his final views and wishes and then comments upon Gabriel's visionary replies, but the dialogue rather awkwardly resembles a formal "news" interview. The voices in this and other dramatized poems in *Heart-Shape* do not resonate sufficiently to provide revelations of character or subtleties of theme, as do later poems of "mixed voice," but the basic patterns of dialogue and dramatic monologue are already present in this early collection of the novice poet.

The more purely personal poems in the collection, the title-piece love "Sonnet to E.," the elegiac tributes to his foster father, "Obituary" and "Rosemary," and some half-dozen straightforward yet self-conscious expressions of emotion (grief, loneliness, love, desire), ring with sincerity but lack the objective correlatives or concrete imagery needed to move the words beyond confessional description to functional art. Contrarily, such descriptive poems as "Sunflowers: Beaubien Street" reveal Hayden's early ability to project meaning through symbolic use of evocative images. The poet's sunflowers function not only internally to suggest the psychic associations of northern ghetto-dwellers with remembrances of a "cruel, sweet . . . Down Home," but the flowers themselves in their vivid, solid tenacity also symbolize the endurance of those who plant them in the urban slum. This poem in its celebration of human will, accomplished through skillful metaphoric extension, compares favorably with later examples in the same general mode, such as Hayden's "Summertime and the Living . . ." and the more recent "Zinnias." Finally, the sheer diversity of the volume defies neat categorization or succinct summarizing. This variety as much indicates the young poet's broad range of interest as it exhibits his early experimentation with technique. In these characteristics,

Hayden's first published collection proved a harbinger of constancy; he would maintain and even expand his range of subjects and themes, and he never forsook his quest for new and improved techniques to express those themes.

Five of the poems from *Heart-Shape* were anthologized the following year (1941) in *The Negro Caravan*. The editors selected "Prophecy," "Gabriel," "Speech," "Obituary," and "Bacchanale" as representative of "one of the most promising of the younger poets."[13] Of course, except for "Obituary," they chose those poems with "black themes" and omitted others of similar or superior quality that are personal, objectively descriptive, or simply "colorless." But then the portrayal of black life by black authors was the announced purpose of those who compiled the *Caravan*. However, these few reprinted poems, in their evident concern with racial history and social justice, do represent rather accurately Hayden's literary preoccupations at that juncture.

The year of his first published collection figures prominently in Robert Hayden's personal as well as professional life. He and Erma were married on June 15, 1940, although his income was negligible and their future prospects were uncertain. Some members of both families, conscious of the hardships facing the young couple, were less than enthusiastic about the marriage, and Robert's foster mother discouraged it directly, but for emotional rather than economical reasons. Her possessive love for Robert simply could not accommodate his love for, and marriage to, Erma. Shortly after the wedding, the pair left Detroit to spend the summer in New York City, where Erma had relatives and the opportunity to study piano at the Juilliard School. While Erma pursued her music studies, Robert did extensive research on the history of slave trade in the United States, using the reference materials at the Schomburg Collection (now the Center for Research in Black Culture) in the Harlem Branch of the New York Public Library. His work stemmed from the desire to write poems about the black struggle for freedom during the slave trade and Civil War eras, an interest no doubt initially derived from his experience with the Writers' Project research.

That summer in New York also brought Hayden into the company of a long-admired "contemporary." Erma knew Countee Cullen, having met him through her uncle when she lived in New York as a youngster. Having renewed the acquaintance during previous visits, she called Cullen, and the famous poet whom Hayden had imitated in his teens graciously invited the young couple to his home. Much to Robert's surprise and gratification, Cullen had a copy of *Heart-Shape in the Dust*, and had even selected his favorite poem from the book, a quasi-allegorical piece titled "The Falcon." Robert was delighted to read the poem at Cullen's request, and certainly the experience of that evening must have sustained Hayden's subsequent struggle to achieve the potential Cullen had discerned in his early work.

Sue Ellen Hayden died shortly after Robert and Erma returned to Detroit in the fall of 1940. Hayden later conjectured that his foster mother seemed just to "give up," as if she lost meaning for her life after she lost control of his life. Erma resumed her teaching duties in the Detroit schools, supporting herself and her unemployed husband. She urged him to concentrate on his research and poetry, and not to let the frustration of joblessness distract him from the goals in which she sometimes had more faith than he:

My wife was teaching in the Detroit public school system and she, being rather advanced in her thinking, didn't see why I shouldn't, since I didn't have a job, stay home and write and not worry about it. But oh, I couldn't do that. I was just worried sick because I didn't have a job. But in 1941 we decided that we would leave Detroit and I would go back to the University of Michigan and get my master's degree.[14]

## The Graduate

The Haydens left Detroit in 1941, relocating in Ann Arbor, where Robert was admitted to the graduate program of the University of Michigan. The timing proved fortuitous, as W. H. Auden was then in residence at the university, teaching a course in the analysis of poetry. Hayden managed to get into Auden's class, which was selectively limited in enrollment. Initially intimidated and yet totally inspired by Auden's brilliance of mind, Hayden flourished under his tutelage. He continued his research on the slave trade at the university library, reading histories, journals, notebooks, ships' logs, and several biographical accounts, including the infamous *Adventures of an African Slaver*.[15] Assisted directly by

Auden's instruction and encouraged indirectly by his renowned example, Robert was writing poems on the Civil War and heritage pieces based on folklore. He spent 1941 preparing the manuscript of poems he called "The Black Spear" for submission in the Hopward Award competition.

Informed by his considerable knowledge of black history and folklore derived from the Writers' Project, the summer research in the Schomburg Collection, and his recent work at the university, the manuscript took shape as Hayden's effort to render an epic of his race, a "blackskinned epic," which depicted their struggle for freedom during the slavery era, the Civil War, and its aftermath. Robert had conceived of this ambitious project after reading Stephen Vincent Benét's *John Brown's Body* (1928). Lighting upon the Benét narrator's acknowledgment that he could not sing the epic from the black man's perspective, that the song would await the arrival of a black poet who could do it justice, Hayden fancied himself that poet, and he aspired to function thusly in "The Black Spear." Although the epic as a project was never completed, its beginnings were auspicious and meritorious enough to earn for Hayden his second Hopwood Award in 1942. Achieving the Major Award in Poetry (with a stipend of five hundred dollars) and receiving the welcome recognition of the judges (including Marianne Moore and John Neihardt) sealed once and for all Hayden's destiny to be a poet.

This Hopwood manuscript also marks the emergence of Hayden's distinctive poetic voice. The prevalent themes naturally adhere to the plan of Hayden's announced "work in progress":

The poems under the title of "The Black Spear" are part of a larger work in progress which has as its theme the Negro people's struggle for liberation and their participation in the anti-slavery movement and Civil War.

The poems presented here may be regarded as a kind of "lyrical synopsis" of the larger work.[16]

But the technique of using mixed narrative voices, evident in some of the earlier *Heart-Shape* poems, recurs with refinement throughout "The Black Spear." The poet's interest in profiling historical personages as "character study" shows through in this collection, perhaps best exemplified in his effort to illuminate the historical significance of Crispus Attucks ("Whereas In Freedom's Name . . .") and John Brown ("Fire Image"). Hayden prominently displays his knowledge of folklore as well as his love of rhythmic and auditory effects in his initial version of "O Daedelus, Fly Away Home." The best poems in the sheaf are those that reveal Hayden's emerging originality; those least effective are in the vein of, and thus too dependent upon, Benét's coverage of similar subject matter.

1942 was a noteworthy year for Hayden in other ways: during that year he became, with Erma, a member of the Baha'i Faith; he received the Bachelor of Arts degree from Wayne State University; and in October, his daughter Maia was born.[17] Although W. H. Auden had by then left the employ of the university, he had maintained a personal interest in his former student, whom he delighted when he came by the Hayden house to see the new baby. Earlier, Auden had helped Robert get a job in the university library, and he continued to encourage his work and advise him on poetics and publication.[18] The library job helped supplement Erma's teaching salary during those first years in Ann Arbor, but Hayden realized he would need something more substantial if he were to support his enlarged family. The "something more" was not much more, but it did allow him to continue his graduate studies. He received an appointment as a teaching assistant at the university when he completed the master's degree there in 1944. He spent the next two years on the faculty of the English Department, teaching freshman courses, and trying to finish those poems that were to have been part of the "Black Spear" collection.

Among them, his "Middle Passage" (1945) and "Frederick Douglass" (1947) best exemplify the use to which Hayden put his years of research, and they illustrate his continuing interest in the heritage of his race. Both poems, in their respective histories of preliminary research, composition, and publication, encapsulate Robert Hayden's midcareer aims and methods. The genesis of the poems can be traced back to the 1930s in his work for the WPA; the deliberate crafting of the initial versions literally took years; the publication record of "Middle Passage," especially, documents the poet's constant effort to revise and improve even his "finished" and acclaimed work. Hayden once described at some length the evolution of "Middle Passage," commenting in the interview on techniques used and effects sought.[19] As in many of his later poems, he achieved a dramatic quality through the use of several diverse voices, speakers-as-participants in thematically significant events. Although he "finished" the poem in 1943, and it first appeared in *Phylon* in 1945, it underwent considerable revision prior to its next printing in Edwin Seaver's *Cross Section 1945*. Hayden again revised "Middle Passage" for inclusion in *A Ballad of Remembrance* (1962). Characteristically, the "Grand Reviser" always intended some day to alter the present ending of probably his best-known work.

## Southern Sojourn; Southern Stay

The title poem of that 1962 collection captures Robert Hayden's response to his first exposure to the Deep South. In 1946, while still on the staff of the University of Michigan, he took his first trip below the Mason-Dixon Line. He traveled to New Orleans to appear on a program at Xavier University in support of a War Bond rally. Hayden, while appalled by the "southern brand" of bigotry and segregation, found himself fascinated with the exotic ambience of the old city. This ambivalent response was further heightened by his recognition of the irony inherent in his reading "Middle Passage" to support a war against tyranny while in the context of an outrageously racist locale. Hayden's meeting with Mark Van Doren as part of the New Orleans experience prompted "A Ballad of Remembrance," written during the following summer.[20]

By then Hayden had "permanently" transplanted himself and his family in the South, since he had in the fall of 1946 accepted a position as an assistant professor of English at Fisk University in Nashville, Tennessee. He was to spend twenty-two years laboring at Fisk, largely unrecognized as a poet of importance, and often little appreciated even in his own local academic community. Not until the 1960s was Hayden regarded by the university administration as a "poet in residence," and not until then did he receive much reduction in teaching duty, much consideration to facilitate his poetic productivity. Like many beginning college instructors in the 1940s, he assumed the traditional burden of undergraduate instruction—an overload of basic courses, with reams of student papers to read, in return for very little pay and less free time.

The immediate physical neighborhood and academic community of Fisk University provided a kind of haven in an atmosphere of Jim

Crow segregation, but the overall contrast between Detroit and Nashville in the 1940s made the Haydens' period of adjustment both difficult and lengthy. For example, at one juncture, to avoid sending their daughter to segregated Nashville schools, they decided on a rather drastic relocation plan. Erma took Maia to New York City, where she enrolled her in a progressive, integrated elementary school. Robert remained at his teaching duties at Fisk while Erma taught music and creative dance at the Little Red Schoolhouse in New York. Of course, ironically, this effort to avoid one kind of disruption in their lives ultimately created another. The extended separations took their toll, and Robert finally took leave from the university to reunite the "divided family" for a year in New York. At the end of that year (1951), they returned to Nashville, where Maia attended regular, albeit segregated, public school.

Since the job conditions at Fisk were less than ideal for an aspiring poet, since the racial atmosphere and provincial attitudes of Nashville at that time were emotionally almost debilitating to a sensitive black poet with an artistic wife and a young, vulnerable family, one may wonder why Hayden chose to go to Fisk in the first place, and why he elected to stay there in the second. Much of the answer lies in how little choice he, or anyone of his race and occupation, had in those days. Except for the brief period of enrollments by returning World War II veterans during 1946–1948, college teaching jobs were as scarce in the 1940s and 1950s as they have been in the 1970s and 1980s. Moreover, black teachers then had considerably less opportunity for employment initially, and for mobility thereafter, than their white counterparts, especially in trying to move from a "black" institution in the South to another kind of school in a different geographical region. Part of the answer also involves Hayden's commitment, his desire to serve his people through instructing and influencing the young blacks in attendance at Fisk. So Hayden and his wife endured the conditions and lived with the limitations by seeking out those with whom they shared views and values: "We found that it was possible to form relationships with people of goodwill who did not have the traditional prejudices. And we found people interested in the arts, people interested in music, and in dance and poetry and so on. And this made a difference."[21]

Through it all, Hayden doggedly persisted in his work and found kindred spirits at Fisk who helped sustain his creative energies. His faculty colleagues included Arna Bontemps, the university librarian, already a noted folkorist, poet, and novelist, who, as a major figure in the Harlem Renaissance, was much more widely known than the young poet. Bontemps and Hayden became good friends as together they pursued their mutual interest in getting told the history of black people in an accurate, equitable fashion. Partially on the basis of his association with Bontemps, but primarily because of his impressive past work and future promise, Robert was awarded a Rosenwald Fellowship in Creative Writing in 1947. These fellowships were supported by the Julius Rosenwald Fund, which between 1913 and 1948 provided a wide assortment of scholarships and fellowships for black scholars, writers, and artists such as Hayden.

## The Baroque Era

Aside from the prestige of being a recipient of the coveted Rosenwald, the fellowship directly assisted Hayden's continuing struggle to write poetry, as well as his effort to promote his own and the work of other poets. While on the fellowship, he and a group of his students sought ways to encourage creative writing at Fisk, and to support black writers in general. In 1948 he joined with another Fisk colleague, Myron O'Higgins, to establish the Counterpoise Series. The two poets organized a small group of students, artists, and interested supporters, raised enough money to finance an initial booklet, and launched the Counterpoise project by publishing *The Lion and the Archer* (1948), a collaborative collection of poems by Hayden and O'Higgins.

In this slim volume, Hayden (the "Lion" of the title, based on the two authors' respective zodiac signs) exhibits fully those characteristics of what he referred to as his "Baroque period." The poems and poetics therein reflect his early fascination with exotic diction and almost metaphysical imagery. Although the "Baroque" elements clearly show Hayden experimenting, striving to develop his own voice, to "outgrow" the influences of others, he in some instances perhaps extended himself farther than the length of his poetic "arms" could reach. *The Lion and the Archer* contains thirteen poems, six of which are Hayden's, notably including his intriguing "A Ballad of Remembrance," an instance of the effective and functional success of the "Baroque." The poem epitomizes Hayden's technique of using ornate imagery and obscure diction for linguistic effect and symbolic texture. He also in this mode employs a preponderance of allusion to extend the richly sensuous detail of what can be visually apprehended, and to convey the ambience of locale and situation. "A Ballad," like Hayden's best work in the Baroque mode, can be summarily characterized as functionally ornate; ornamented, but not just ornamental. Selden Rodman, reviewing *The Lion and the Archer* in the *New York Times*, praised both Hayden and O'Higgins as "gifted poets," and cited the "experimental vigor of these poems."[22]

As the "Lion" of the collection, Hayden curiously shifts the metaphor in his concluding poem, entitled "The Lion." In it he portrays himself not as a lion, but as the "Archer," the one who would cage and tame the lion of art. He expresses his commitment to poetry through indirect reference to his religious faith, as he metaphorically figures the meshing of creative urge and controlled craftsmanship as a holy activity, where the demands of art challenge both sense and soul.

This vision, although rather obscurely rendered in "The Lion," proved prophetic as applied to Hayden's artistic destiny during the ensuing decade. He, as "captive prophet-king in byzantine disguise," continued the struggle to practice and perfect his art, without finding much applause. Eight of his poems appeared in *Poetry of the Negro, 1746–1949*, a substantial anthology edited by Langston Hughes and Arna Bontemps in 1949, but Hayden generally found recognition and time for writing both equally rare commodities. Finally, he won a Ford Foundation Grant, which allowed him relief from classroom duties at Fisk and the opportunity for travel and writing in Mexico during 1954–1955.

Hayden took with him an unfinished manuscript of current work, hoping that the change of scene and the "leisure" time would help him in revising "old" poems while he accumulated cultural experience as material for new ones. Having majored in Spanish in college, he had little problem with language barrier; intensely interested in "everything Spanish," he lived in Mexico City with a Mexican family during much of the sabbatical year. For that interim Hayden fully indulged his "lust for life," his consuming curiosity about people and places. Yet, as he also later reported, he again experienced the nagging feelings of isolation and alienation, that complex irony of identity whereby he felt like an outsider even while touching and being touched by the lives of others. It was after the year in Mexico that Hayden began to invoke publicly his "favorite personal paradox" that "no place is home for me, therefore every place is home."[23]

Nevertheless, the travel and cultural experience proved personally and professionally beneficial; Hayden returned to Fisk with his creative energy renewed, and with notes, sketches, and ideas for future poems "steeping" in his mind. The poems in manuscript he had taken to Mexico soon appeared as *Figure of Time: Poems*, printed in the Counterpoise Series (#3) shortly after his return in 1955. The poems in this brief collection are perhaps no more indicative of Hayden's self-image and perspective at this stage in his career than is the poet's choice of title, which paraphrases a segment of a speech in Shakespeare's *Othello*, where that tragic hero in soliloquy portrays himself as fate's victim, as a man destined to be scorned through the ages. Hayden continued to judge himself rather harshly, dissatisfied with his accomplishments and frustrated with the difficulty of trying to pursue his craft while earning a livelihood, doing justice to his teaching and students, as well as coping with the "normal" day-to-day demands of marriage and family life. The poet found that even these relatively benign forms of adversity impeded his progress, limited the amount if not the quality of his poetic output.

Consequently, his work during this period was erratic in productivity, although the product was consistently polished in craftsmanship. Out of "worldly distractions," personal pride and overly harsh self-criticism, Hayden, in spite of total commitment and hard work, added comparatively little to his canon of completed works during the 1950s. The history of his "A Ballad of Remembrance" serves as a good illustrative case in point. Between its initial publication in *The Lion and the Archer* (1948) and its "final form" in *A Ballad of Remembrance* (1962), where it appeared as the title poem of only his second substantial collection of poetry in over twenty years, Hayden revised "A Ballad" at least fifteen separate times. The span of fourteen years between publication of collected poems (1948–1962) seems inordinately long for a poet so clearly committed to his art. The external demands on his time and energy, combined with his unrelenting self-demand for perfection, partially explain what appears to be a lengthy hiatus in his work.

## National Neglect; International Recognition

On the other hand, the "gap" also measures to some extent the critical neglect Hayden suffered during this period. Although he regularly placed poems in American literary journals and small press magazines; although his poems were being translated into Serbian, Japanese, Spanish, Italian, Russian, and German, and even periodically broadcast by the British Broadcasting Company, no one was paying much attention to Robert Hayden in the United States during 1955–1960.

Hayden's work found an appreciative audience in England and Europe during the late 1950s and early 1960s due largely to the interest and support of two individuals. The support of Dr. Rosey E. Pool, an eminent Dutch scholar, derived from her research dating as far back as the early 1920s. She "discovered" Countee Cullen in 1925 while a student at a Dutch university working on a paper on "Contemporary American Poetry," and from that point she began to assemble what she considered the best work of America's black poets. Her interest in such work heightened as the European audience expanded. Black poetry, with its themes of protest, resistance, and endurance against oppression, appealed by analogy to the underground literati and "ordinary" partisan fighters in Occupied Europe during World War II. Pool herself joined the Underground Resistance against the Hitler occupation of Holland, was imprisoned, escaped, and lived hidden for nineteen months until the Liberation. By the early 1950s Dr. Pool's collection of works by those she considered the best black poets included Robert Hayden in the front ranks; she began to champion his cause by prominently including selections of his work in her frequent readings to live audiences and over radio in London.

Among Pool's readings was a program entitled "Black and Unknown Bards," after the now well-known poem by James Weldon Johnson. The selections she presented that evening at the Royal Court Theatre in London in the fall of 1958 included

Hayden's paean to Harriet Tubman, "Runagate Runagate." Pool soon thereafter published the poem and the others on the program as *Black and Unknown Bards*, a collection, according to its preface, "not meant as a cross-section of the writing of Negro poets, but an historical reflection of the position of the Negro people in America and examples of their mordancy, wit and imaginative power as natural endowments, deepened by adversity and sharpened by their parallel existence and evolution in White America."

Dr. Pool first met Robert Hayden in 1959 while in the United States on a Fulbright Travel Grant. A subsequent tour of American colleges in 1963 brought her again to Nashville, where she read her favorite poem, Hayden's "Runagate Runagate," at a poetry recital in which he participated on the Fisk University campus. Hayden in later years cited Dr. Pool's admiration of that poem as the prime cause for his "resurrection" and revision of "Runagate."[24] Ultimately, Pool lauded Hayden as the "Negro Poet Laureate" in a *Negro Digest* article in June 1966. During the decade prior to that culminating tribute, however, Hayden's reputation in his own country remained largely "underground." Herbert Hill, who during that era came to Fisk to give a lecture, then assured Hayden, "You have the best underground reputation of any poet in America." Hayden's response: "I wish it would surface; I wish it would surface."[25] Ironically, Rosey Pool, after herself functioning "underground" during World War II, and in admiration of Hayden's poetic portrayal of Harriet Tubman and the Underground Railroad, finally brought Robert Hayden to the surface on an international scale that ultimately came to include his own country. It was Rosey Pool who read Hayden's work publicly at every opportunity in Europe, who caused his poems to be broadcast over the BBC; it was she who included a representative segment of Hayden's poetry in her *Beyond the Blues* (1962), an anthology of "New Poems by American Negroes."

Perhaps most importantly Rosey Pool had also in the late 1950s brought Hayden's work to the attention of a young London scholar named Paul Breman, who had been interested in black poetry since 1947. Breman shared Pool's discernment of Hayden's importance; because of Robert Hayden, Breman's activity as a collector developed into a commitment as a publisher. He honored the "new" poet by choosing Hayden's collection, *A Ballad of Remembrance*, as the initial volume for the Heritage Series, a sequence of black poetry books that Breman inaugurated in 1962.[26] Initially contracted for the book by Breman in 1959, Hayden spent the next three years meticulously working over the materials that American critics had ignored. *A Ballad* both justifies the poet's arduous labor and indicts the negligent critics. Moreover, the book brought Hayden the international acclaim that would eventually translate into national recognition.

In *A Ballad of Remembrance* Hayden brought together revised and improved versions of some of his best work from the 1940s and 1950s such as the title poem, "Middle Passage," and "Frederick Douglass." He also reflected recent travel experience and current interest in several poems that correlate regional history and geographic atmosphere, primarily those in response to the South and those now known as the "Mexican poems." Significantly, the collection contains as well several dramatized portraits of fictional, historical, or family personages. Of the thirty-six poems presented in four separate sections, roughly two-thirds could be categorized under the general heading of "people and places." Of those, about a dozen portray vividly, through either descriptive narrative or dramatic monologue, historical figures (Nat Turner, Frederick Douglass, Bessie Smith), fictional characters ("Witch Doctor," "Mourning Poem for the Queen of Sunday," "Perseus"), or family members ("The Burly Fading One," "Those Winter Sundays," "The Whipping").

The latter poems Hayden would later call "memory poems," as he explained his need to recapture and yet artistically objectify people and events from his past. That urge, and his continuing interest in dramatized portraiture of unique, striking characters, whether "real," imagined, or compiled, would again manifest themselves in subsequent works to become prominent features in the full evolution of his poetic voice. However, in *A Ballad*, except for portraits of real and imagined blacks, and "memory poems" such as "Summertime and the Living . . .", few of the "new" poems in the collection touch on themes inherently racial in subject or theme. Hayden tried hard during this period to "escape" being limited to the role of racial spokesman, as he produced works that sometimes reflected black history or culture, but were not dependent upon a racial identity of author or perspective.

Given the validity of the foregoing generalization, yet more irony of circumstance accompanies Robert Hayden's gradual rise to recognition in the years following publication of *A Ballad of Remembrance*. Like Paul Breman, Rosey Pool's promotion of black poetry was not limited to Robert Hayden alone or to American black poets only. Their mutual interest spanned oceans and continents as they assembled, selected, and published black poets of all nationalities whose poetic expressions of "Negritude" they believed ranked with the best "anglophone" contemporary writing. Thus when in 1966 the First World Festival of Negro Arts was organized and held in Dakar, Senegal, to emphasize "Negro artistic parity" with other races worldwide, Rosey Pool served on the jury for the literary prizes, and Robert Hayden was among those being judged. Through her expert "witnessing," the concurrence of the jury chairman, Langston Hughes, and the acknowledged superiority of *A Ballad of Remembrance*, Robert Hayden won "the *Grand Prix de la Poesie*," the ultimate honor for a black author of "a book of poetry published between January, 1962, and September, 1965, which has not received any other prizes or distinctions."[27] Of course, had Hayden's book received the attention it warranted in his own country, he might not even have been eligible for the Grand Prize in Dakar. Even more ironically, the black poet who regarded himself as a poet who happened to be black, the poet who was almost ignored in the United States while he worked to transcend the limited way society and literary critics tended to view black artists, had been judged the best poet of blackness in the world. The citation read, in part ". . . a remarkable craftsman, an outstanding singer of words, a striking thinker, a *poete pur-sang*. He gives glory and dignity to America, through deep attachment to the past, present and future of his race. Africa is in his soul, the world at large in his mind and heart."

Dr. Pool's tribute to Hayden and her praise of his poetry ("originality, creativeness, disciplined inspiration, craftsmanship in the handling of the raw material . . .") appeared in *Negro Digest* soon after the Dakar World Festival. While the piece could not be called sustained literary criticism, it does represent the first published critical response to Hayden's poetry in the United States. Another significant "after effect" of the Dakar prize resulted in the first publication of a book of Hayden's poems in his own country since *The Lion and the Archer* in 1948. October House, under the direction of David Way, brought out *Selected Poems* in 1966. Publication in New York City by a "commercial" press does not guarantee expanded readership, given the limited distribution of small-press publications, but it generally does cause a book to be reviewed more widely than "hinterland" printing. Such was the case with *Selected Poems*. While the few reviewers found much to praise in the collection, perhaps the very existence of the four reviews themselves could be taken as the most favorable response to Hayden's slow rise to the surface. Gwendolyn Brooks added her prominent voice to the complimentary chorus of the Dakar Festival jury in her review in *Negro Digest* (October 1966). Another reviewer, writing in *Poetry*, lumped together "Three Recent Volumes" to discuss the book; David Galler, after acknowledging that "Hayden is as gifted a poet as most we have," goes on to portray Hayden as the victim of the paradox of black poets—either limited by the inescapable subject matter of race, or driven by that subject matter to "sentimentality or hyper-erudition." Galler closed his review by claiming that Hayden was "saddled with both."[28]

So while Hayden strived to write poetry of merit which addressed inclusive human themes in forms based on a universal artistic aesthetic, white critics began to notice him only by judging him as a black poet limited to a racial perspective. Ironically, at about the same time, the militant voices of the black activists of the 1960s began to attack him for his refusal to subjugate his art to their social, political and moral aims. In a typical instance, during a Black Writers' Symposium conducted at Fisk University in 1966, several participants took vociferous issue with Hayden's assertion that there should be no difference in the criteria for judging art, whether the artist be black, white, or whatever. This stand did not endear Hayden to those who could have given him more exposure to a black readership just beginning to discover the polemic "rap verse" directed specifically to that expanding audience. But Robert Hayden refused to allow the dictates of militant rhetoric or the emerging "black aesthetic" to shape his work, just as he simultaneously refused to be trapped in the "literary ghetto" seemingly reserved for him by the white establishment. Thus even as the long overdue recognition began to come, it came in the form of paradox.

In spite of it all, Hayden endured, striving to juggle his teaching, research, and writing, while trying to take advantage of the increasing opportunities for expansion of his "public" self. Self-promotion never came naturally or easily for Robert Hayden. While

committed to his art to the extent of risking alienation from a
sizable segment of other black writers, he had no patience with
personality cultists, those who would support celebrity while largely
ignorant of its basis. Hayden continued in the late 1960s to accept
invitations to read his poetry in the knowledge that accommo-
dations were often minimal, audiences were frequently small, and a
heckler or two in the guise of black militancy was a real possibility.
As scrupulously conscientious in fulfilling social and professional
obligation as he was determined to forward the cause of poetry,
Hayden's forays on the "circuit" brought him a reputation for
personal and artistic integrity. Occasionally, the readings
themselves, as "performances," could be awkward affairs, as
Hayden struggled to adjust his poor vision to inadequate lighting
and unfamiliar surroundings. However, audiences unfailingly
responded to his quietly humane presence and the muted drama of
his reading. In sum, Hayden preached poetically what he practiced
personally; racial distinctions evaporated into the warmth of human
dignity—few in his audiences were left unmoved by Hayden's
unique articulation of human experience.

With exposure, discernment, and appreciation of his insightful
skill came limited but welcome new challenges. The first of many
"residencies" came as he spent the summer of 1967 as Poet-in-
Residence at Indiana State University. During the previous year he
had begun compiling materials for a new anthology of black poetry;
it was published in 1967. In that volume, Hayden's apparent lack of
discrimination as an editor more clearly reflects his values as an
artist. *Kaleidoscope: Poems by American Negro Poets* contains
representative selections from forty-two poets, ranging from Phillis
Wheatley to Leroi Jones, from Paul Laurence Dunbar to Ted Joans.
The range of subjects and techniques conveys both individualistic
and universally applicable responses to experience, the "black
experience" within the larger framework of the general human
condition. He simply collected what he considered the best
American Negro poetry, choosing, as he commented on the dust
jacket, "poems for their literary value rather than for their
significance as an expression of social protest or racial struggle."

Hayden also in 1967 accepted the appointment as poetry editor
of *World Order*, the quarterly journal of the Baha'i Faith. He
continued in this post until his death, never wavering in the editing
premises and standards he professed succinctly in an introductory

essay preceding a ''Portfolio of Recent American Poems'' printed in the spring 1971 issue. Therein he likened the making of a poem to a prayer, the result of which can affirm the humane and spiritual. This he put in opposition to nonserious art of only politically utilitarian value, but he would not ''censor'' those manifestations of decadence as their creators would him. Indeed, Hayden's descriptive summary of the character of those poems he selected for that issue to ''attest to the vitality of contemporary American poetry'' apply as well to the work he would produce in the ensuing decade: ''Here are poems that express the malaise and disjunctions of our times as well as poems that reflect personal experience or honor transcendental values.''[29]

# The Return

At the height of the civil unrest and antiwar protest of the late 1960s and early 1970s, Hayden traveled throughout the country, giving poetry readings, observing the effects of violence and disorder, and experiencing alternating periods of emotional distress and consolation in response to it all. One aspect of consolation was Hayden's return to the University of Michigan during 1968 as a visiting professor of English. During that brief interim he found more recognition and more opportunity of national scope than he had previously derived from his long association with Fisk. That year he joined Derek Walcott for a joint poetry reading at the Library of Congress, and remained in Washington, D.C., to record some of his poems for the Library of Congress Archives and to appear with Walcott in a documentary film broadcast on public television channels. The film's title, ''Middle Passage and Beyond,'' suggests its nature, an historical summary of the black experience since slavery, supplemented by poetic expressions of that experience as rendered by writers like Hayden, Walcott, and others.

Perhaps the most significant result of the year at Michigan was Hayden's subsequent move from Fisk back to the permanent employ of his alma mater. While he returned to Nashville in the fall of 1968, he scarcely ''settled in.'' He spent the spring semester as Bingham Professor at the University of Louisville before resigning his position with Fisk, and then moved on to Seattle to spend the

summer as a visiting poet at the University of Washington before
reporting to Ann Arbor to accept the appointment as professor of
English at the University of Michigan in the fall of 1969. In spite of
this "peripatetic professor" role, or perhaps because of it, Hayden
could not escape what was happening throughout the land. His effort to cope with public problems in a personal way strained his
faith, but could not finally shake that faith or alter his artistic
outlook.

## The Mourning Time

As the country suffered through assassinations, racial unrest, urban riots, protest demonstrations, the dissension brought on by an
unpopular war, and the war itself, Robert Hayden suffered compas-
sionately, empathetically, personally. In time he managed to objectify much of his anguish through his art; the fruition of this
painful process came in 1970 with the publication of his *Words in
the Mourning Time*. The central title poem of this slim collection
(twenty poems in four sections) exemplifies the somber tone that
pervades much of the poetry included. "Words in the Mourning
Time" chronicles the strife that was rampant in the country's events
and mood during the period, and Hayden candidly acknowledged
that the poem tended to be as cathartic as it was artistic. Yet he
concludes the cryptic descriptions of chaotic moral disorder not with
dire prophecy or self-righteous clucking, but instead with a note of
hope, a statement of desperate faith, whereby the present turmoil
could be reconciled as a harrowing progression toward the ultimate
achievement of human understanding and brotherhood.

Although the other poems in the collection are diverse in subject
and mode, several echo this conjunction of anguish and faith. The
disparate subject matters of black history ("The Dream"), regional
lore ("Locus," "On Lookout Mountain"), biography and character
portrayal ("El-Hajj Malik El-Shabazz," "Aunt Jemima of the
Ocean Waves," "Lear Is Gay"), technology in an age of alienation
("Zeus over Redeye," "Unidentified Flying Object"), and the
vagaries of life versus the permanence of art ("Monet's
'Waterlilies,' " "The Lions," "October") seem to share a common thematic bond in that so many of the poems emphasize
human despair, endurance, and the possibility of transcendence. A

dark era depicted as a "mourning time" forms the core of the volume, but the informing spirit of the poetic voice suggests also an eventual end of mourning, an enduring through a temporal tragedy.

*Words in the Mourning Time* provided its author with an outlet for his compassionate grief, and yet gave its readership an artistic response to the times. Critical response, both in degree and nature, showed that Hayden's long overdue recognition had begun to take shape. Julius Lester, a former student of Hayden's at Fisk, justly claimed in a review of the book that Hayden was "one of the most underrated and unrecognized poets in America."[30] Yet in that same year (1971), the volume was favorably reviewed in *Saturday Review*, *Prairie Schooner*, and the *Library Journal*. Curiously, and an indication of the neglect to which Lester referred, these reviews appeared a year *after* the book had been nominated for the National Book Award, a year *after* Hayden had received for it the Russell Loines Award for Distinguished Poetic Achievement from the National Institute of Arts and Letters.

## Blossoming from the Dark

While Hayden did not complete the new poem specifically commissioned by the Phi Beta Kappa chapter of the University of Michigan in time to include it in *Words in the Mourning Time*, he gave the first public reading of "The Night-Blooming Cereus" before that group on March 21, 1970. The poem, for all its clarity of vision, represented for Hayden a struggle of enormous proportion. Shortly after the publication of *Words*, he felt he had shot his poetic bolt—that he had no more to say, and no way of saying it, anyway. The struggle to complete "Cereus," to fulfill his obligation to the commission, thus became a test of his artistic endurance.

Again, a combination of inner strength and external obligation prompted the gradual progression of his work. Although he had found time in 1971 to edit the poetry section of a new anthology of black literature, Hayden had completed to his satisfaction precious few poems since the revision of "Cereus."[31] Later that year, Paul Breman asked him to provide enough new work for a limited edition to mark the tenth anniversary of the Heritage series. Resultantly, Breman printed in 1972 150 copies of *The Night-Blooming*

*Cereus*, a pamphlet of eight gemlike Hayden poems. In addition to the title poem, *Cereus* includes the masterful "Peacock Room" and the cryptic haiku "Smelt Fishing," among the poems composed and arranged to dazzle the reader with the imagery of brightness, light, and darkness. A second edition soon followed, as did the flow of Hayden's rejuvenated productivity and academic activities. Among other things, he discussed his work at some length with a young editor named Paul McCluskey; those conversations appeared as Hayden's first published interview in *How I Write / 1*. He served on the poetry staff at the Breadloaf Writers' Conference in August 1972 and closed out the year by editing the modern American poetry section of *The United States in Literature*.

## Ascent Achieved

Over the next couple of years, Hayden began to attract a modicum of critical attention as he continued teaching at the university, working on new projects, giving poetry readings, and filling visiting poet positions. John O'Brien interviewed him and several other black authors in doing a doctoral dissertation, later publishing the revised text as *Interviews with Black Writers* in 1973.[32] That same year, Hayden's work received general critical coverage in an article of note, "Robert Hayden's Use of History," by Charles T. Davis, and the *College Language Association Journal* printed two articles on specific Hayden poems.[33] Meanwhile, Hayden was hard at work on those poems which would be published in 1975 by Liveright Press in New York.

As it turned out, in view of the subsequent response to the book, and the acclaim of its author, Hayden had prophetically titled *Angle of Ascent: New and Selected Poems*. The phrase "angle of ascent" appears in Hayden's allegorical folk tale adapted from a short story by Gabriel Márquez called "A Very Old Man with Enormous Wings." Hayden titled the poem "For a Young Artist" to signal the allegorical import of the story, suggesting his (or any artist's) struggle for understanding, achievement, and recognition. In his latest work, and in the public and critical response to it, Hayden by 1975 truly had achieved "the angle of ascent."

The new poems in *Angle* suggest also the completion of an evolutionary cycle begun in the 1930s. Hayden, who began his poetic career writing subjectively and sometimes sentimentally about his personal life, had for many years "distanced" or entirely avoided personal and biographical poems about his immediate family and his inner emotional responses to them. In 1975 he reconciled his psychic subjectivity with his artistic ability; he returned, if only briefly, to subjects and themes of personal history. He introduced *Angle of Ascent* with "Beginnings," an account of his family ancestry, almost as if he were announcing an intention to complete the biographic cycle of personal lyric. The other new poems verify the unique quality of Hayden's mature poetic voice, just as those "selected poems" in the volume trace in a representative fashion the evolution of that voice.

Within a few months of the publication of *Angle of Ascent*, Hayden's peers recognized his enduring record of progress and his culminating achievement. Nominated by William Meredith, the Academy of American Poets elected Hayden their 1975 Fellow, with a stipend of ten thousand dollars. In his home state, recognition came that year in the form of an honorary Doctor of Letters degree from Grand Valley State College. Finally in 1975 national recognition caught up with, and in a sense surpassed, the international recognition inherent in the 1966 Grand Prize awarded in Senegal. In response to that award, Rosey Pool had presumed to proclaim Hayden the "Negro Poet Laureate." Ten years later, Hayden accepted the appointment as the Consultant in Poetry to the Library of Congress, America's closest equivalent to, or counterpart of, England's laureateship.

Prior to making the move to Washington, D.C., and taking up his duties in the consultant post, Hayden spent much of 1976 fluctuating between the production of new poems and the receipt of honors for them. For example, the Detroit Institute of Arts commissioned him to write a poem on the incendiary abolitionist, John Brown. The poem, the writing of which led Hayden through a *déjà vu*–like re-researching of the topic, would in 1978 be included in an elegant portfolio of screenprints after the *The Legend of John Brown* exhibition of Jacob Laurence's twenty-two original gouaches presented by the institute from October 14 through November 26, 1978. Hayden's commission for "John Brown" turned out to be one of the limited number of the portfolios, a clear example not only of "art for art's sake," but of art as the direct reward for art, an

arrangement that proved happily appropriate to Hayden's poem
and poetics. Again in 1976 the Michigan Chapter asked Hayden to
compose and read the Phi Beta Kappa poem. He responded in April
with "American Journal," a perceptive vision of America in its
bicentennial year, an intriguing glimpse at the essence of his native
land and its people from the unconsciously ironic perspective of an
alien persona.

Typically consistent with his personal warmth, Hayden evoked
personal as well as institutional encouragement during these years
of increasing renown. Hayden had in the early 1970s formed a
lasting bond of mutual understanding, shared artistic values, and
professional support with Michael S. Harper, a black poet-scholar
whose present prominence bespeaks his importance to the future of
American poetry. Harper himself during the decade of the 1970s
proved as peripatetic as Hayden in the forwarding of the art
through preaching its gospel across the geography while unceasingly
practicing his craft. Through Harper's affiliation with Brown
University, that institution had the good sense to recognize both
Harper's astute judgment and Hayden's artistic achievement by
conferring upon Hayden his second honorary degree in June 1976.

When he assumed his duties as the Consultant in Poetry in
September 1976, Hayden resolved to "open up" the office and its
activities as much as possible. He took in stride the initial publicity
emphasizing his unique status as the first black poet to be appointed consultant, because he knew his reputation had finally
"surfaced" not because he was black, but more probably in spite of
it, and because he realized that those peers who had recommended
him for the position (notably including his predecessor, Stanley
Kunitz, and his successor, William Meredith) had held a genuine
respect for the merit of his work over the years. When the media
mayhem diminished, Hayden began to concentrate on a sustained
effort to invite poets of all backgrounds, locales, "schools," and
degrees of prominence to read their works at the library, thereby
adding their recorded readings to the Archive Collection. Between
that "pet project" and the official duties of scheduling readings
and programs through the year, in addition to responding to re-
quests for interviews and readings of his own, Hayden had to make
a conscious effort to "reserve" some time for his own research and
writing. That he managed both the administrative and the creative
with equal ability can be discerned from the events of the following
year.

If Hayden's initial appointment as consultant was unprecedented for a black poet, his reappointment for another year in the office was equally distinctive. He began that second year by participating in a series of poetry readings at the Folger Shakespeare Library in conjunction with the presidential inauguration. Some of the poems read on these occasions would soon appear as part of the special emphasis on black literature provided in two successive issues (fall and winter 1977) of the *Massachusetts Review*.[34] Hayden's editors at Liveright Press, not surprisingly, were eager to publish such works as "American Journal" and "Elegies for Paradise Valley," a moving revisitation of the people and ambience of Hayden's birthplace. But, as a commercial press, Liveright could not accommodate a collection of such limited volume. In view of these circumstances, and sensing the importance of getting Hayden's latest work in print, Michael Harper established Effendi Press and published *American Journal* in 1978 in a limited edition of one hundred numbered and signed hardbound copies and one thousand paperback copies.

Many of the poems in *American Journal* represent work completed by Hayden during his tenure as consultant. While "Names," a poignant, first-person account of the poet's life-long search for identity, is the most intensely personal of the thirteen poems in the collection, "Elegies for Paradise Valley" may be ultimately the most self-revealing. Hayden's deft skill in psychological portraiture can be seen in "The Rag Man," and in his "A Letter from Phillis Wheatley," a "psychogram" sketch in an epistolary mode. His interest in technology and its effects on modern man, first demonstrated in "Zeus over Redeye" (1970), shows through again in "Astronauts." Finally, the sustained revelatory monologue of the alien persona in "American Journal" disguises Hayden's direct voice yet reveals his true feelings about himself, his countrymen, and the times.

"How it Strikes a Contemporary," an address delivered on May 8, 1978, as Hayden's final "performance" in his capacity as consultant, took the form of a dialogue of mutual antagonism between two personae, "The Poet" and "The Inquisitor." Hayden characterized his personally created "Devil's Advocate" by suggesting that his Inquisitor at various times bore similarities to "certain acquaintances of mine who feel it is their duty to see that I keep both feet on the ground"; "certain professors I have endured who have tried in vain to convince me that Shakespeare said it all and therefore I should accept the fact that I was born with too little

too late''; ''These self-appointed guardians of poetry''; and
''certain criticasters for whom my blackness is so dense they can
never see their way through or beyond it to me as a poet.'' The
Poet's running debate with the ''cynical and querulous'' Inquisitor
provides Hayden a dramatic format for self-justification and for a
defense of poetry and poets in general. Hayden realistically allows
the Inquisitor to score some points, but the Poet wins the debate in
a conclusion that summarizes Hayden's artistic credo: ''Let there be
poets and more poets—just as long as they are poets. For poets too
are the keepers of a nation's conscience, the partisans of freedom
and justice, even when they eschew political involvement. By the
very act of continuing to function as poets they are affirming what is
human and eternal.''

While returning to Ann Arbor late in the summer of 1978,
Hayden sustained injuries in an automobile accident, compounding his physical problems of failing eyesight and high blood
pressure. As he recuperated at home that fall, frustrated by the
psychological effects of his physical condition, he found some solace
in the nomination of *American Journal* for the National Book
Award. Although he eventually had to content himself with
runner-up recognition, losing out to James Merrill's *Mirabell: Books
of Number*, the sponsoring American Academy and Institute of
Arts and Letters belatedly invited his membership. He was inducted
into the academy the following spring.

He quite literally had to battle for his life during the winter in
order to be able to travel to New York for the induction ceremonies.
He underwent major surgery for cancer on three separate occasions
through those months, and although the doctors' prognosis was
optimistic, Hayden in the early months of 1979 was weak and somewhat dispirited. But, characteristically, he called again upon his
inner resolve and drew strength from Erma's positive outlook, both
of which had sustained him over the years. When his health allowed
him to resume a portion of his duties at Michigan, Hayden took
measures to facilitate his creative output in the face of his physical
limitations and the welcome but overwhelming demands upon him
by the same literary establishment and general public that had for
so long benignly neglected him. He of necessity limited his public
readings, hired a young graduate student as a personal secretary,
and acquired a virtual beast of a typewriter to type oversized print so
he could read and revise his own manuscript drafts with less
difficulty.

Liveright meanwhile urged him to add more work to the *American Journal* content so that they might reprint those poems and publish the new work in the same collection sometime in late 1979. Hayden somehow found the energy not only to continue writing, but to continue exploring untried themes and techniques. His inexhaustible originality and disciplined craftsmanship continued, paradoxically consistent in their ascending angle of improvement; he never said the same thing twice, and each time he said it better than before. Some topics grew out of new, unsought happiness; others derived from the poet's need to objectify and express "old" agonies. The happy coincidence of UNICEF's proclaiming 1979 as "The Year of the Child" and the adoption of a child by Hayden's daughter and son-in-law established a context for the bittersweet comparison of his own joy in his grandson and the plight of disadvantaged children around the globe, as expressed in the touching yet unsentimental poem he called "The Year of the Child (For my Grandson)." Yet he also poetically struggled with his inner demons again in such poems as "Ice Storm" and "The Tattooed Man." He once more vicariously returned to Paradise Valley to recall childhood Saturdays at the movies in "Double Feature." Earlier in the year he had literally returned to his old neighborhood to retrace his steps up Beacon Street, followed that time by a director and a camera crew in the production of a television documentary on Hayden's life. Later that January day he would reminisce in an interview format in front of those same cameras in a different setting, a posh hotel suite provided by an organization that would present him with a distinguished-citizen award.

Hayden worked diligently through the summer of 1979 to put into their final forms the new poems for the Liveright collection. Finally, in December, he was ready; he took a week off, flew into New York, and hand-carried the manuscript to his editors. He stayed over to see old friends, browse in bookshops and stationery stores, and simply relax after a semester of teaching, writing, and obliging more people than even he realized. Slowly but surely regaining his strength, he looked forward to a sabbatical spring semester during which he could get at unfinished projects such as "The Snow Lamp" and a poem on Josephine Baker.

The new year began with a climactic conclusion of the long trek from Paradise Valley obscurity to national prominence. President and Mrs. Carter honored Hayden and several other recognized

American poets with an invitation to a "White House Salute to American Poetry" on January 3, 1980. One may ponder what reveries Hayden indulged in as he and Erma waited in the reception line to be introduced to the president and first lady—how did this compare to that long-ago evening with Countee Cullen? Was the Senegal honor more gratifying in its individuality, or did group honor in his own country mean more? What would "Ma" and "Pa" Hayden and his "real" mother think of this? Hayden later reported his pleasure at the Carters' graciousness, and the personal gratification he enjoyed in being one of the relatively small number of poets asked to read that evening. He read "The Night-Blooming Cereus" to those gathered in the East Room, with Mrs. Carter and Mrs. Mondale in attendance. He recalled telling Erma, "It's been a long way from the ghetto to the White House, but it was worth it."[35]

While Hayden was basking in this national limelight, his faculty colleagues at Michigan, prompted by one of their number who had been a student at Fisk during Hayden's tenure there, began organizing their own tribute to the "local" poet. Jointly sponsored by the Center for Afroamerican and African Studies and the Eva Jessye Afro-American Music Collection at the university, "A Tribute to Robert Hayden" was conducted on February 24, 1980. The participants, either through their attendance in Ann Arbor or their written tributes, included Michael Harper, who gave the main address, Gayle Jones, who read from Hayden's work, Gwendolyn Brooks, Margaret Walker Alexander, Dudley Randall, William Meredith, Naomi Long Madgett, Darwin Turner, Nikki Giovanni, Alice Walker, Herbert Martin, and a host of other friends and admirers, along with prominent officials of several universities.

Ironically, Hayden himself was unable to attend his own tribute. He had been suffering from viral influenza through the preceding week, and although he vowed to attend, whether sufficiently recovered or not, Mrs. Hayden prevailed. He nevertheless received friends and well-wishers in his living room for a brief time that afternoon after the tribute, although he was not up to joining them at the banquet in his honor that evening. Quite unexpectedly, he took a turn for the worse the following day, was hospitalized and died that evening (February 25, 1980) of an embolism in his lungs. In retrospect, those who attended the tribute and talked with Hayden on that day agreed that the poet had seemed to sense something, that he was saying goodbye without their realizing it. Hayden was interred later in the week in a modest grave in Fairview Cemetery in Ann Arbor; the tributes to his memory would follow later, themselves followed by the widening recognition and full appreciation of the power of his poetry.

## Yet Does He Marvel

In his poetry, and in his conversations about poetry, Robert Hayden frequently turned to one of his favorite themes—the effort to distinguish appearance from reality, that search for truth, whereby to illuminate and enrich human experience. One cannot read much of Hayden's poetry without concluding that this ongoing pursuit of truth was for him more than a favorite theme; it was perhaps closer to a "ruling passion." The corpus of his work over the years—indeed, his career as a poet—attests to the acute awareness with which he perceived reality. He continued to marvel at life; he remained in the conviction that a higher reality resided beneath the surface reality, and that an artful expression of this higher reality would give an added dimension to the ordinary experience of his readers. This combination of faith and talent made him a truly marvelous poet.

Yet the literary critic who would trace the evolution of Hayden's poetic voice, who would analyze and explicate his over four decades of work, must begin by identifying with the speaker in "American Journal," as that otherwordly analyst expresses the frustration of trying to generalize about an ever-changing phenomenon:

> an organism that changes even as i
> examine it   fact and fantasy never twice the
> same   so many variables

Anyone trying to "capture" Robert Hayden has the same difficulty. Even in the fruition of his artistic goals, at the height of his poetic powers, Hayden did not content himself with self-satisfaction. Because he relentlessly pursued a constantly changing reality with untried themes and innovative poetic techniques, he scarcely could be expected to lie still under the critic's microscope.

And yet it is precisely because Hayden continued throughout his career to be intrigued with life's "fact and fantasy" that his expressions of reality will continue to intrigue his readers and critics.

## Chapter Two
# Heart-Shape of the Lion
''The Poetry Is the Thing''

As patient and accommodating as Robert Hayden was with biographical queries, he preferred to subordinate his personal life in discussions of his poetry. Hayden believed that while biography could inform criticism, it could not substitute for it. Nevertheless, his autobiographical poems reveal much about his development as a poet. Since he began his career writing personal lyrics, then refrained from purely personal utterance during midcareer, and finally returned more frequently to his own biography as the poetic subject matter that would culminate his growth as an artist, the origins of that cycle can be discovered in early poems classifiable as ''personals.'' Other poems in perhaps his favorite category, ''people and places,'' yield a clearer understanding of his interest in characterization and symbolism—subject topics that also indicate much about Hayden's affinity for narrative variety and dramatic monologues. Several early poems based on lasting interests in black history and culture, the topics with which Hayden has been often oversimply identified, demonstrate the full range early in his career of the growth and power he would experience as a poet. Finally, those poems contemplating transcendental themes such as art, religion, and the nature of reality, when taken together, provide insight into Robert Hayden's artistic values and his spiritual concerns.


## Personals

*Heart-Shape in the Dust* (1940) illustrates both the strength of Hayden's emotional response to loved ones and the early limitations of his ability to express those responses artistically. ''Obituary,'' written to honor the memory of his foster father, William Hayden, perhaps typifies this strength of feeling, although the poem reveals

some weakness in expression.[1] Hayden eulogizes his deeply
religious foster father with recollections of the Bible lessons the
young poet learned as a child sitting at his father's knee. The
speaker recalls those stories in colorful, romantic detail: "Cymbals
and roses / And bronze and myrrh, / Flame and thunder / Those
stories were." These bright images contrast dramatically with the
elder's stern moral code, and with his exhortation to "shun evil."
The limit of young Hayden's poetic ability is evident in his failure to
exploit these contrasts. The muted acknowledgment of memory is
touching in its filial reverence, but the potential for dramatic tension goes unheeded, or at least untapped. Hayden closes the poem
with a brief account of his father's quiet, peaceful death, offered as
proof of the virtue of his life. So while "Obituary" remains a sincere
tribute, the poetry often shows more sentiment than skill. For example, some of Hayden's diction seems chosen more for rhyme
than reason, as in these lines describing Bible stories in summary:
"Of Samson's strength / Columnar and faulty / And Lot's wife
standing / Forlorn and salty."

"Rosemary," another elegiac poem in memory of William
Hayden, although as intensely personal as "Obituary," achieves a
correlation of form and function that makes it superior to its
companion piece. In "Rosemary" Hayden uses spareness of detail
and brevity of length to reinforce the rather commonplace notion
expressed:

> He never lived for us
> Until he died;
> We never knew him
> Till he moved
> Beyond the need
> Of our too laggard knowing. (37)

The speaker avers in only six lines comprising only twenty-three
words that since his foster father was never appreciated until he
died, he never "lived" until he died. The family never knew him
until too late. Similarly, the short poem is over before (just as) the
reader becomes engaged in the topic. Randall Jarrell would later use
a similar format to extend the thematic impact of his "The Death of
the Ball Turret Gunner" (1942), but Hayden's short poem of long

remembrance augurs the emotional and artistic commingling he would later refine through austere restraint.

Hayden's most clearly identified autobiographical love poem, written in the bloom of youth, indicates again the shortcomings of some of those initial personal lyrics. In "Sonnet to E." (31) Hayden recounts his flirtation with suicide, and contrasts that impulse with the saving grace of Erma's love. However, he portrays death not as a feminine persona in competition with Erma for his love and loyalty, but as "dear father, friend, and victory." The speaker also recalls times when despair made death seem a "balsam-handed lord." The central point of the sonnet concerns disillusion; the speaker can no longer be fooled by death's charming masks because love has taught him to see more clearly. Although Hayden personifies both love and death, neither is personified clearly; neither is set in a figurative opposition on a consistent basis. Hayden seems randomly to have selected and arbitrarily used the English sonnet form. The Shakespearean rhyme scheme does not provide an octave-sestet break, a division of the Petrarchan form that could have signaled the transition from despair to revelation. Hayden derives no advantage from the quatrain format or the concluding couplet, but rather arbitrarily breaks line ten with ellipses to describe the comforting lesson taught by love as a tutor of "generous wisdom." Although "Sonnet to E." genuinely testifies to the benevolent power of love, Hayden's use of form and figuration lacks coherence.

*Heart-Shape* contains several other no less intense lyrical expressions of deep emotion, "personals" not identifiably autobiographical as revelations of particular relationships. These poems are more nearly assertions of strong feeling unaccompanied by subject or object. As such, they tend to be abstract in their expression and obscure in imagery. For example, "Grief" (34) is "Like hail blown over / Summer grass," while love perceives beauty in "Three Leaves" (35) as the "nightingale music / Of her face. . . . Whose face is a chorus of dark stars." The beauty perceived by love in "Orison" (36) becomes something both elemental (fire, air, water) and amorphous. Consequently, the speaker-lover out of fearful anxiety pleads not to be forsaken by something elemental enough to be addressed, but too amorphous to be tangible. On the other hand, "An Old Song" (38) presents a straightforward plea for love by a speaker who had formerly denied himself love because he was foolish enough to believe that he needed only spiritual communion with nature. These poems as love lyrics express concomitant emotions of fear, loneliness, and anxiety, but too many of the poems seem rather abstractly pathetic in their romantic self-indulgence or masochistic angst.

Hayden's emotional fervor renders his sincerity self-evident, but the artistic merit of such early lyrics is sometimes inversely proportional to the depth of feeling sustaining them. Thus in his early career, Hayden's personal poems frequently betrayed his artistic aspiration. This disjuncture between art and emotion can easily be attributed to many sources: his youth, the early influences of his reading, his domestic situation, his personal insecurity and sensitivity. More important, his conscious decision to forego the personal lyric, to refrain from speaking in this voice in the poetry written after *Heart-Shape in the Dust* marks the beginning of his development as a poet of importance. Significantly, he chose this direction during his formative years, as he purposefully sought to fulfill the demands of poetic art. In the consciously experimental work represented in *The Lion and the Archer* (1948), Hayden completely eschews personal lyric as he seeks "psychic distance" to accommodate objectified art. He would continue to practice his "distancing" well into his mature career.

## People

Hayden's interest in people as subjects with potential for poetic drama begins to show through in the varied "voices" created in his *Heart-Shape* poems. The "fleshing out" of people as portrayals of dramatized psyches would come later, but a few "set pieces" in *Heart-Shape* are precursive. For example, "Old Woman with Violets" (54) succinctly enlivens an image of humanity as a symbol of life itself:

> Quiet and alone she stands
> Within the whirling market-place,
> Holding the spring in winter hands
> And April's shadow in her face.

As a harbinger of the seasonal cycle, the old woman retains her simple personal identity in this haiku-like poem. Hayden locates the old woman, "quiet and alone," amidst the activity of the "whirling market-place," thereby emphasizing the primary symbolic contrast between the woman's age (the winter) and her violets (the spring, "April's shadow"). By using an old woman in conjunction with first-blooming violets, Hayden encapsulates the recurrent rebirth of life in the spring, and suggests the natural cycle of life. Moreover, the old woman, who holds spring in her "winter hands" and "April's shadow in her face," personifies youth of the spirit. With simple but striking imagery, Hayden transforms an otherwise obscure old woman into a universal, timeless symbol.

Comparable perhaps only in genuine human interest as the principle motivating the poet, Hayden's tribute to Bessie Smith in *The Lion and the Archer* exemplifies his developing ability to create memorable dramatic portrayals of ordinary and extraordinary people. In "Homage to the Empress of the Blues" he daringly blends the intellectually exotic diction of his "Baroque period" with the blues rhythms and tones emblematic of Smith's performances, in order to explain her effect upon black audiences. As brief and simple in structure as the cause-and-effect premise of a blues song, "Homage" moves twice in succession through a three-part movement: Because unfaithful love causes the kinds of misery an oppressed people could relate to, Smith's renditions of "Faithless Love / Twotiming Love Oh Love Oh Careless Aggravating Love" provided her audiences a vicarious escape from miseries more mundane. She in "yards of pearls" "flashed her golden smile, and sang" the blues as a form of solace for those whose lives were shaped by fear.

Through this progression of fearful misery experienced, sung, and thereby exorcised, Hayden pays homage in terms exactly appropriate to his subject. Bessie Smith becomes a presence, a phenomenon, not merely a personality or portrait. The poet's logical premise ties the singer to the lives of her audience; Hayden claims that she "shone that smile on us and put the lights to shame" because their lives were so in need of that special light. She emerges as a symbolic personage representing both the desperation and the hope of those with whom she is identified. Hayden thus accomplishes a dramatic vividness of the individualized portrait, and posits potentially transcendent symbolic implications. In these features "Homage" resembles his subsequent dramatic portraits of "special" people—living, dead, fact or fiction, from racial heroes to scoundrels to fondly remembered relatives.

## Places

Robert Hayden's early travels, coupled with his ambivalent attitude toward place ("No place is home for me, therefore every place is home."), led him to diverse locales, and led him to write about them. Yet none of his "place poems," from the earliest to the latest, is an exercise in static description. He dramatizes even what might be called "loco-descriptive" poems by populating them with living people or by symbolically interpreting natural surroundings.

"Sunflowers: Beaubien Street" from *Heart-Shape* (12) serves as a good illustration. Descriptive of the physical setting and cultural ambience of the neighborhood of his youth, the poem captures the emotionally charged recollections of rural southern Negro life and contrasts those "created" memories with Hayden's own memories of urban ghetto poverty. Hayden evokes these images and projects these emotions through the artistically simple expedient of using the lowly sunflower as a central symbol, as the linkage in a free association of similar yet contrasting images. Ghetto dwellers, themselves "transplanted" from South to North, Hayden likens to the sunflowers these people have planted in the inner-city slums. As "dark votaries of the sun," Hayden's people subconsciously see in the sunflower's shape and color "sun-whirled, tropic tambourines," "chain-gang heat and shimmering pines," "the sun / Fixed in the heavens like Ezekiel's Wheel." Hayden's sunflowers epitomize the faith and resolve of those who plant them, and they thus symbolically testify to the strength of these people in their endurance of adversity. This early example of Hayden's "place" poetry is loco-descriptive at first glance only; "Sunflowers" defies simplistic categorization as the poet celebrates "those dark ones" who "find mere living sweet." In its fusion of symbolic image and realistic descriptive detail, and as a place poem which is more about human traits than geographic locale, "Sunflowers" anticipates more sophisticated examples in this mode.

Robert Hayden's own reverse migration from Detroit to Nashville in late 1946 prompted another poem based on geography, but located in symbolic irony. For "Magnolias in Snow" (in *The Lion and the Archer*) he juxtaposes conventional symbols (magnolias suggest the South, snow suggests the North) to express his altered perception of the South. Seeing the magnolia trees in a rare snow-covered southern landscape evokes in him an unexpected response. The snow, which reminds the speaker of the North and "home and friends," ironically "warms" him in the sense that by appreciating the changing beauty of southern natural surroundings he can "compensate for things I must forego / if I would safely walk beneath these trees." By responding aesthetically to this "baroque / surprise," Hayden finds natural beauty a compensation, a comfort to offset the emotional deprivation he, as a "displaced" black poet, experienced in the South of an earlier era. The poem, like "A Ballad of Remembrance," reveals Hayden's mixed response to the atmosphere and geography of the South, where he often felt alien and isolated even while exulting in the beauty and rich heritage of that locale.

Like "Magnolias," "A Ballad of Remembrance" is a place poem with personal overtones, but both describe the speaker's response to location in symbolic and thus objectified terms. Hayden called "A Ballad" his baroque poem; a few detractors would label it a classic example of "hyper-erudition."[2] They failed to appreciate Hayden's crafted effort to suggest the atmosphere of old New Orleans in the 1940s, complete with its tarnished elegance and stifling racism. Hayden phrases his attraction-repulsion response in images that convey the confusion of "poison jewels," of "love and hate among joys, rejections." The poet's brief catalog of a representative black populace makes symbolically graphic the milieu of this "schizoid city." In New Orleans the speaker, almost as an alien intruder, encounters "Quadroon mermaids, Afro angels, black saints," "the Zulu king," "the gun-metal priestess," and "masked Negroes wearing chameleon / satins." In contrast to their exotic diversity, these projections of the speaker's psyche are unified in their demand of compliance with their respective exhortations:

> Accommodate, muttered the Zulu king,
> toad on a throne of glaucous poison jewels.

Love, chimed the saints and the angels and the mermaids.
Hate, shrieked the gun-metal priestess
from her spiked bellcollar curved like a fleur-de-lis.

Even in their surrealistic disguises, these "characters" clearly represent the emotional options confronting blacks in a racist society. Torn among the conflicting urges to "accommodate" in return for tainted reward, to martyr oneself through love and saintly forgiveness of oppression, or to return hate for hate, thereby engendering self-hate, Hayden welcomes the association in New Orleans with "meditative, ironic, / richly human" Mark Van Doren. Van Doren's friendship helped Hayden gain perspective, enabling him to speak with his "human voice again" in rejecting those "minotaurs of edict" confronted earlier in his own psyche. So he concludes the poem by characterizing New Orleans as a state of mind. Through the cathartic progression of this example of "crafted confusion" Hayden makes possible yet another application of the same adjectives with which he characterized Van Doren—both Hayden and his "A Ballad of Remembrance" are indeed "meditative, ironic and richly human."[3]

## Heritage

Except for the inherent yet indirect racial basis of "Magnolias" and "A Ballad of Remembrance," no poems of black history or culture appear in *The Lion and the Archer*. Contrarily, of the forty-seven poems in Hayden's earlier *Heart-Shape*, at least twenty address rather directly the subject of blackness. Practically all of these poems exhibit a sociological orientation as they recount injustice and plead for racial justice, equality, and human brotherhood. Many of them are derivative, if not imitative of noted contemporary socially conscious black poets such as Claude McKay, Langston Hughes, Countee Cullen, and Arna Bontemps. Those poems most original are not "new" in subject or theme, but innovative in Hayden's use of narrative variety in creating dramatized "voices." A brief survey of representative poems, including those probably "inspired" by contemporaries, and those exemplifying Hayden's experimental use of verbal echo or dialect, clarifies the specific distinctions between the two general categories.

Many poets of the Harlem Renaissance sensed and expressed analogies between Christ's crucifixion and the lynchings of innocent blacks. Among others, Claude McKay and Langston Hughes wrote protest poetry in this vein.[4] McKay's sonnet "The Lynching" (*Harlem Shadows*, 1922) metaphorically hints at the analogue, but thematically contrasts the purposeful, redemptive meaning of Christ's death with the totally meaningless death of a lynching victim. Hughes in his "Song for a Dark Girl" (1927) speaks through the "Dark Girl," a mournful singer who laments the death of her lover, hanged on a "cross roads tree."[5] The grieving girl finds love "a naked shadow / On a gnarled and naked tree," as she in despair forsakes praying to a "white Lord Jesus."

Hayden's "Religioso" in *Heart-Shape* (39–40) seems almost a composite of these two poems he most probably read during his high-school or college days. Like those earlier examples, "Religioso" highlights the disparity between Christian redemption and racial injustice. Like Hughes before him, Hayden uses a "Brown Girl" as the speaker in the opening segment of his two-part protest piece. "I. Brown Girl's Sacrament" begins with the invitation of the Eucharist ("Eat of His Body") as an epigraph. Hayden then in two successive tercets compares Christ's physical death ("the bruised body / . . . Lynched on the hill of Calvary") with her lover's murder ("charred April body / of my lover, / Swinging from a tree in Dixie!"). The second stanza of this section is again prefaced with a communion imperative, "Drink of His Blood," but the second section of "Religioso" makes the emotional and moral parallels between Christ and the lynched man more explicit. The new speaker, a racial and moral spokesman, directly addresses Jesus to claim that all blacks know Christ's agony by virtue of their own suffering, just as all black mothers know Mary's pain in loss.

In his reference to Mary and the ironic conclusion of the Eucharist, Hayden may also reveal his familiarity with Hughes's "Ballad of Mary's Son" (*The Langston Hughes Reader*, 1958). Although Hayden in this work owes a clear debt to at least McKay and Hughes, he derives only limited benefit from "borrowed" premises and parallels. He elaborates on the same ideas found in his "sources," but in so doing he sacrifices economy and thus achieves less impact than either McKay or Hughes. Perhaps the most striking difference is Hayden's avoidance of a disillusionment with Christianity, which seems implicit in "The Lynching" and is quite explicit in "Song for a Dark Girl." "Religioso" concludes in a pious tone that doggedly retains that traditionally close association between black faith in Christian religion and the racial experience of innocent suffering.

## Echoes in Imitation

In his early "heritage poems" Hayden often unknowingly falls or consciously plunges into a similar process or pattern: he imitates his predecessors in subject matter, theme, or even figuration, but alters their perspectives and changes their conclusions. For example, his "We Have Not Forgotten" (10) seems reminiscent of Countee Cullen's "From the Dark Tower" (1927), and similar to Arna Bontemps's "A Black Man Talks of Reaping" (ca. 1927).[6] All three poems address deprivation and suffering in terms of the agricultural images of plowing, sowing, fruition, and harvest. Cullen views his people in the present, where their efforts (tending "agonizing seeds") are thwarted (others reap what they plant). Yet his speaker looks forward in desperate conviction ("We shall not always plant while others reap"). Bontemps takes a sweeping look back through history ("I have sown beside all waters in my day") and then limits his perspective to the present, in decrying the status quo where their planting benefits others while blacks get only the gleanings. His speaker expresses the frustration of a people cheated and driven to "feed on bitter fruit."

Hayden in "We Have Not Forgotten" also adopts a past perspective, but for the primary purpose of honoring past planters. His speaker emphasizes the faith and hope of those black ancestors whose prayers and songs ("songs your anguish / Suckled") amount to a racial legacy. The poet then shifts the perspective and mixes the metaphor to equate those songs with the soil in which present hopes can grow. He again alters the imagery to make that figurative soil the literal land of America, claiming that this land will at long last yield freedom. Such a future harvest depends on present love for nourishment and on past example for inspiration—the spirits of those ancestors walk beside them as they plow. Because Hayden applies his harvest imagery unevenly, he does not present a sustained analogy, but his poem nevertheless seems logically coherent. The seeds of faith will bear the fruit of freedom because the present generation can find inspiration in the example of their predecessors. Perhaps the success of Hayden's poem can be found in its fulfillment of poetic purpose; he honors black ancestors in gratitude for their legacy of faith, whereas Cullen and Bontemps protest social conditions by citing the self-evident lack, or perversion, of present harvest. In any event, the three poems, when considered together, suggest that Hayden as an apprentice imitator could often successfully compete with those who provided him models for emulation.

He less successfully echoes Claude McKay's "If We Must Die" (*Harlem Shadows*, 1922) as a statement of resolve in the face of racial persecution. Hayden's "We Are the Hunted" (46) evidences clear similarities in language, logic, and figuration, except the "We" in Hayden's poem are fleeing from "lantern-eyed hounds" and "the hooded posse," rather than being attacked by McKay's more figurative "mad and hungry dogs," "the murderous, cowardly pack." Hayden portrays a people in flight, running while yet maintaining a strong belief (a belief "more relentless than the savage pack") that refuge awaits "somewhere just ahead."

"We Are the Hunted" consists of two five-line free-verse stanzas connected by a linkage line. In the first stanza Hayden assembles the persecutors, and then with the transitional "We run, run, run" he sets the pursuit motif in motion. McKay instead urges defiant resistance, a fight to the death. Understandably, McKay's imagery depicts persecution as more graphically frightful and threatening. Hayden's characteristically subdued protest emphasizes a determination to endure. In that emphasis he could be rejecting McKay's hypothesis, saying, in effect, "We need not die, but we must persevere." Unfortunately, the structure of the poem inadequately supports that message, since the emphasis on fleeing in fear logically undermines the claim of "relentless" hope. Not until the final revision in the early 1960s of his masterful "Runagate Runagate" would he convincingly equate physical flight and faithful perseverance.

Hayden elsewhere in *Heart-Shape* again adopts and modulates the voice of a contemporary to speak as a racial spokesman in the manner of Langston Hughes. Hayden's "The Negro to America" (26) and Hughes's "Let America Be America Again" (1938) share

similarities of direct address and moral assertion in keeping with
similar polemic objectives.[7] Both claim America has failed to live up
to its promise, but Hayden seems less willing than Hughes to
acknowledge a past promise gone awry. Instead Hayden refutes as
mere propaganda both traditional symbols and present pretense.
As an indictment of America, the poem makes racial injustice and
democracy mutually exclusive in reminding the audience that as
long as blacks are denied, "you [America] are not / Democracy."
His speaker, an "everyblackman," contrasts the false emblems of
freedom and democracy (the flag, the statue of liberty, legionairre
[sic] parades, the DAR) with the reality of racial persecution,
punctuating his text with the refrain, "you are not / Democracy."
The "Negro" of Hayden's title assumes an essentially external
perspective in presenting America as seen through the eyes of world
opinion. From that perspective the poem exerts moral pressure
through an emotional appeal. For all its justified moral
indignation, however, "The Negro to America" is finally more an
impassioned speech than a poem. Little wonder then that its author
looked back in bemusement at his poems of this ilk, and reductively
proclaimed them "speechifyin'."

In his youthful attempts to equal his "betters," Hayden was not
immune to their fascination with the taboo subject of interracial
love as a source for provocative verse.[8] While Hayden's treatment of
this theme could lead him to borrowed imagery and untried
allusiveness, it could also push him toward melodramatic excess.
"Southern Moonlight" (16) shows the general influence of Jean
Toomer's *Cane* (1923) and the particular inspiration of Toomer's
imagery in "Blood Burning Moon." Hayden reverses the racial
identities of the lovers (white woman, black man) and inverts the
moon symbolism, but to little poetic avail. Hayden's moon casts
threatening light on a forbidden assignation; his white female
speaker asks the moon to help her by not shining upon her and her
lover. Toomer's moon seems more deeply symbolic as an omen of
the destructive forces over which victims of their own passions have
no control.

"Diana" (43) also concerns the destructive effects of interracial
relationships, but in its excess this "exercise in southern
mythology" borders on the lurid. Self-conscious of his allusive
premise, Hayden anounces that mythological basis parenthetically
as the poem's subtitle, and goes poetically downhill from there. To

describe an encounter between a white temptress and her black "victim," Hayden uses the point of view of the enemy, those "lords of purity," who manifest their racist outrage in brutality. The irony of this modern Diana as "chaste harlot" in "her venereal virginity" gets lost in the confluence of violent and erotic language. The "keepers of the white rose" scream for punishment of the worst kind ("Flay, rend, burn") while oblivious to the temptress's role in the affair:

> Nor report
> the eager invitation of her breasts
> and how her thighs—
>
> . . . . . . . . . .
>
> were quivering towards him,
> imploring the hard, male touch of him.

For all their flaws, these two poems have positive, if not totally redeeming features importantly indicative of Hayden's future growth. In both he uses the narrative device of personae, daringly disparate from his personal stance. The speaker in "Southern Moonlight" is the white woman who asks the moon to "put out your light" to hide forbidden love. Hayden's assumption of lynch-mob mentality and language provides an ironic narrative perspective in "Diana," but even that collective persona suffers from "overwriting."[9] Nevertheless, the voice in "Diana" is clearly not Hayden's. These poems stand as early if crude examples of his tendency to create personae, using indirection to engender dramatic interest, even while seeing himself as a direct racial spokesman.

## Original Voices

Other poems in *Heart-Shape* better illustrate this mode, wherein Hayden combines an accurate ear and a polemic urge to echo individualized blacks speaking of group concerns. These concerns as poetic subjects are not original, but Hayden's use of verbal echo to convey them represents an innovative, yet natural trend in his earlier poems of black heritage and culture. While "Gabriel" (23–24) presents mixed voices in a dialogue format, the historical hero speaks not in an "authentic" voice of the original Gabriel

Prosser, but in poetically stylized verse, with Hayden in the foreground as interviewer, and not very far in the background as ventriloquist. However, the language does express Prosser's visionary personality and his historical significance in the black struggle for freedom. Hayden's later "Ballad of Nat Turner," a dramatic monologue, could be viewed as the refined, superior counterpart of "Gabriel."

Compared to "Gabriel," Hayden more skillfully phrases his contemporary protest in poems like "Shine, Mister?" (42). Speaking in the dialectal colloquialisms of the ordinary unemployed black man, he indirectly yet effectively describes and thus protests the working and living conditions of Depression-era Detroit blacks. Even the skilled laborer cannot find work in local factories ("Ford ain't hirin— . . . Briggs is firin . . . Man at Cadillac / Said: Gwan back home"), or in government recovery programs:

> Asked for a shovel
> On the W. P. A.
> Man said: Uncle Sam
> Ain't handin out today.

The speaker stands on the street with the "no-job blues," oscillating in alternate stanzas between the frustrations of joblessness and luckless gambling ("Went an played me a number / But it wouldn't come"). Reduced to shining shoes, "Tryin to make a dime," the speaker's appeal, "Shine em up, mister, / Shine?," echoes through the poem. He summarizes his plight and Hayden's protest in the closing lines, "Lawd, a po workin man / Has a helluva time." The profundity of Hayden's theme may be on the same level as the mundane interests of his speaker, but the apt language fits both speaker and subject. This early "dialect verse" demonstrates Hayden's innate knowledge of what he called "folk language," an idiom he would continue to use as a powerful poetic resource throughout his career. With such speech patterns he characterizes; with character he dramatizes; with drama he extends theme. In retrospect, one senses that these "trial flights" in verbal echoing were the origins of his polished dramatic monologues of mid and late career.

The persona in "Bacchannale" (44), while literally a "blood brother" of Hayden's shoe-shiner, responds differently to his frustration of similar cause. Down, and out of work, he decides that since he "Can't laugh" and "Don't wanna cry," he is "Gonna git high," because

> A little likker
> O a little gin
> Makes you fergit
> The fix you in.

But even as he resolves to drink his troubles away, he worries beyond that "Bacchanale": "Wonder what I'll do when / Ma lush-money's gone." Although the speaker simplistically rationalizes his drunkenness through self-pity,

> There must be joy
> There's gotta be joy somewhere
> For a po colored boy
> This side of the sky,

the sorrow seems as genuine as its implied cause well beyond just unemployment. Hayden implies that the man's misery can be only temporarily relieved by alcohol. But since the poem vividly portrays "miseryin on" through the speaker's individualized voice, those protest implications are subtly embedded, rather than laid on with a heavy hand.

While "Shine, Mister?" and "Bacchanale" protest social conditions not unique to blacks then or now, "Ole Jim Crow" (51) expresses the angry frustrations of blacks oppressed by the legalized racism of the not-too-distant past. Again, Hayden's speaker employs the vernacular common to the many being oppressed by "Ole Jim Crow." In his homely wisdom this "common man" figures these discriminatory laws in "literal" terms—Jim Crow is a hateful bird who has "done built him a nest" all over the land, especially "down south," where "ole Jim Crow's / a-flappin an a-croakin / in every tree." By transforming the real injustice from abstract restrictive laws into a tangible object (an old bird) for abuse, the speaker can vent his frustration and retain his dignity through a resolve to act. As his anger builds ("Gittin mighty mad. . . . Just let him keep on a-messin with me!"), the speaker vows imminent action:

Gonna feed him
some goopher-dust
first thing you know.

This ultimate threat, to use "conjure" in the form of "goopher-dust," superstitiously believed capable of causing or curing evil, seems appropriate for such a formidable foe as Ole Jim Crow, whether just an old pervasive bird or implacable, legalized prejudice. Thus the poet very effectively fuses folk language and lore with moral outrage. Through the folk idiom his speaker functions as a collective voice in protest against discrimination, a voice that threatens retaliation in cultural rather than polemical terms. Hayden achieves in these three poems through vocal inflection what he, even as "The People's Poet," could not accomplish through the overt preaching of such poems as "Speech" (27).

Although in the same rhetorical mode as "Speech," Hayden's "These Are My People," the tour de force that concludes *Heart-Shape* (56–63), contains within it the varied voices seen separately in previous poems. Therefore this lengthy "speechifyin" poem has intrinsic interest for its narrative dexterity. Hayden subtitles his work "A Mass Chant," and opens by speaking directly as the black poet, calling the poem "my song, / a sorrow song, / a dream song, / a hope song, / a black man's song," thereby announcing both his subjects and primary moods. By dividing the "song" into Roman-numbered sections, Hayden distinguishes subtopics and some of the separate speakers; other "voices" he makes distinct with bold-faced print.

In the initial section he uses an external anonymous speaker to pose rhetorically the questions, "who are your people, / what are your people, / that I should listen, / that I should remember?," in establishing a premise for the subsequent survey of black social history. The poet answers these questions in diverse ways; all answers stress the plight of an oppressed, disinherited race. Hayden characterizes "my people," whose "great, dark, myriad hands" built a land from which they are evicted, as "sun-lovers" cast into the darkness of ghetto disease, despair and death. He links the opening generalizations to more specific descriptions of grim ghetto life by inserting a snippet of another voice—a street-corner activist urging, asking, "O humble-down brothers, / when you gonna rise, / rise up free / in a land of the free?"

The subsequent description itself could be subtitled "Spring in the Slums," as Hayden sets off the season of reborn life and hope with details of hopeless ghetto life. This hopelessness is the common lot, and the poet emphasizes its pervasiveness through a catalog of residents, from the young "pale mulatto girl," "singing a song of despair," to "black old men and women / [who] sit on decaying porches / remembering, remembering, remembering / the lost bright Aprils of their strength." Among "painted women" and black children playing gangsters, arrives the street preacher, who comes with "his sad, bright heaven-talk / like a wilted bouquet of sunflowers":

> Hebben, hebben, hebben, Lawd
> Oh, brothahs an sistahs, don yo wanna go?
> Won't have to humble yoselves no no
> in hebben, hebben, Lawd

But his incantations work no more changes in these people's lives than does the seasonal cycle. For these people there is no spring, in any connotation of that term.

Hayden reenters the poem as historical narrator to sketch briefly the descent from the glory of ancient black civilizations to subjugation, and then focuses on contemporary black labor. He sustains the "myriad hands" motif in blending the vernacular of a modern black laborer's lament with excerpts from the lyric of the folk ballad, "John Henry." These images of "strong hands" seem derived from Richard Wright's "I Have Seen Black Hands" (1934), and the folk vernacular recollects Sterling Brown's work in *Southern Road* (1932), but Hayden puts his own stamp on these materials through a deft musical melding of traditional and contemporary work songs.[10] The poet abruptly inserts into this fuguelike flow a dialogue between a white labor boss and a black worker, as a means of reminding his audience that "black hands idle in the sun / handcuffed to their own blackness" because of racial prejudice. The dialogue is as brief as its message is blunt:

> Move on, black boy
> no jobs today.
> Boss, ma kids is hongry,
> an the rent's to pay.
> Move on, black boy
> you ain't ofay.

The narrator also summarizes that John Henry has been deprived of his hammer, and replaced by a "black crap-shooter with his hand on his gun." He points an accusing finger at America as he moves from North to South in the coverage of his song, as he moves from the theme of deprivation to that of outright human destruction.

Evoking grotesque pictures of lynch murders and the sounds of "lynch-lust voices," the speaker calls particular attention to the 1931 Scottsboro case as paradigmatic of racial injustice. In retelling the story of "nine black boys . . . riding / on the long black train / of despair and pain," Hayden proclaims their innocence, but most importantly he notes the "million voices" raised in protest against the Scottsboro injustice. This unified voice he regards as a natural, irresistible force that will bring future change. The "song of hope" culminates in a resurrection thesis, first applied figuratively to an individual lynch victim ("O burned black body / on the tree of pain, / you shall be born, / be born again"), and then expanded literally to predict racial equality and freedom through a "new birth."

Hayden closes the poem by stressing that unity of spirit with chantlike repetition: as the black people go "marching / marching / marching / up from the slums / and toward tomorrow," he calls for human brotherhood, and asks his white audience to join that march. The "dark hands" reach out in appealing,

> O white brother,
> won't you march with me?
> Take my hand
> and march with me.

"These Are My People" derives, of course, from the same spirit informing Langston Hughes's "Let America Be America Again" and Margaret Walker's "For My People" (1937), and in many features is dependent upon these prior amalgams of pride and protest. Yet even in the midst of producing imitative verse, Hayden was learning his craft, beginning to find his own voice, his own artistic avenues. The "heritage" poems in *Heart-Shape* thus have interest and value not because the work is of consistently high quality or because the poems show how derivative Hayden was at first, but because they provide a basis for assessing the mode and degree of his development thereafter.

# Transcendence

Two early poems in those first collections separated by eight years of development can suggest the artist's credo in the state of evolution. The first, "Essay on Beauty" in *Heart-Shape* (29), expresses a priority system that subordinates art to race, whereas the later "The Lion" in *The Lion and the Archer* elevates art to the realm of the spiritual, where Hayden commits his talent to human, rather than strict racial concerns. This later testament does not reverse or repudiate the priority emphasized in "Essay," but rather subsumes both elements of that earlier dichotomy.

Hayden perhaps takes his inspiration and title from Shelley's "Hymn to Intellectual Beauty," but in another sense he "takes off" from where Countee Cullen left off in his famous sonnet, "Yet Do I Marvel" (*Color*, 1925). Cullen's concluding couplet, "Yet do I marvel at this curious thing: / To make a poet black, and bid him sing!," leaves his speaker amazed that God could expect a black poet to articulate lyric joy or freely express artistic imagination at the exclusion of his racial status, his "black experience." Hayden seems to be picking up that thread in "Essay." Perhaps his speaker even addresses the same God, since he directs his comments to the ultimate agency or source of beauty by referring to "your beauty's passionate burning" and "your beauty's pentecostal tongues." In his address Hayden's speaker asserts that, for him, beauty fades when compared to the suffering and struggles of his racial kind. The final triplet restates the dichotomy and reinforces the priority:

> There is no beauty that can cry to me
> More loudly than my people's misery,
> No beauty that can bind my heart and they not free.

Unlike Cullen's speaker, Hayden's concludes resolved and committed. He may "sing," but not merely for the sake of the beauty of the song. The lustre of artistic beauty can never outshine the "blood-bright legends" of his people.

As an artist, Hayden learned what Cullen knew; art and racial commitment can coexist; one form of dedication need not displace the other. As Cullen in his sonnet implicitly noted, any black poet would find it difficult to "sing" in celebration of life and beauty while oblivious to the suffering of his race, or even to "sing" of his own blackness without an element of melancholy or rage in his song. However, "sing" is so general, so expansive a term that rather than connoting exclusion, "sing" suggests inclusion, and more importantly, transcendence. The black poet can still articulate his blackness, can express his unique racial experience while singing his humanity. "Yet Do I Marvel" acknowledges the difficulty of achieving transcendence, but Cullen's poem also claims the possibility.

Hayden between 1940 and 1948 discovered that same possibility, partially from his own artistic experience and partially in response to his faith in the humanitarian principles of the Baha'i Faith. The statement of possibility is at once his emerging credo and his poem, "The Lion." In that poem Hayden speaks as the archer who has trapped a lion. Although he does not have his imagery under control, and the allegorical implications are murky as a result, an allegorical reading is not only possible, but necessary.[11] Having caged the "emperor of anger," the archer stands before the cage where the lion sleeps. Hayden's visual and aural images suggest a lion tamer's act in a circus atmosphere. The archer, carrying a whip, and wearing a "multifigured coat," approaches the cage with "parakeet panache." In brief, Hayden's archer is Hayden himself, the artist who would tame the lion of art. He suggests the challenge of art, and his humility in the face of that challenge through the cryptic "parakeet panache" with which he approaches the task. He sees himself as a parakeet in a lion cage. Acknowledging the applause which prompts his entry through "danger's door," the archer opens that door while blaring trumpets bolster his courage to a lionlike level appropriate to the challenge.

But once inside the cage, his perception alters; he sees "a beast of Revelation, / a captive prophet-king / in byzantine disguise." The challenge of artistic commitment becomes a spiritual experience. In a 1972 "Statement on Poetics" Hayden prosaically articulated this conceptual connection between his craft and his faith: "I think of the writing of poems as one way of coming to grips with inner and outer realities—as a spiritual act, really, a sort of prayer for illumination and perfection."[12] As the lion leaps through the turning fire, the archer's soul exults; he cries, "Holy Holy." The lion, in leaping to his commands, becomes the "gold shadow of my will." Hayden the poet creates art as a prayer, and he in turn is created (brought to spiritual life) through his commitment to that highest good. The lion in art is "dire beauty that creates / and tethers my desire."

Hayden thus describes his revelation, his personal recognition that art and the creative process can exalt the soul, can function as prayer. This spiritual interpretation of his total commitment to his craft accommodates his emotional need to address human concerns and express the beauty he seemed to forsake in "Essay on Beauty." "The Lion" traces a progression in Hayden's artistic experience; what he originally conceived a dazzling display for audience approval came to be a soul-exalting prayer on behalf of the all-inclusive audience of humanity. Hayden reaffirmed that vision twenty years later by converting "The Lion" into a more austere, pointed statement of the relationship between art and the artist, retaining both the title and the central idea for "The Lions" in *Words in the Mourning Time* (1970). The consistency of that view is evident in a 1977 interview statement on the same subject:

. . . in the writings of Bahaullah, the prophet of the faith, it's clearly stated that the work of the artist—and by artist I mean anyone engaged in the art of poetry or whatever—the work of the artist is considered a form of service to mankind and it has spiritual significance. If the work is done with great sincerity and devotion, and, of course, with knowledge, you know, then it is considered really a form of worship and a form of service to mankind.[13]

## Technique in Transition

During the era in which Hayden was developing this requisite knowledge, the distance from *Heart-Shape* to *The Lion and the Archer* also spans his changing practices in the technical aspects of his craft. Virtually every element of prosody reflects a shift, suggests a trend. His habits in prosody during those early years move from sometimes almost slavish adherence to traditional modes of rhyme and meter, through patterns imitative of contemporaries, to a more original, organic freedom to correlate subjects, themes, and prosody. For example, he uses traditional rhyme schemes and metrical patterns for well over half of the forty-seven poems in *Heart-Shape*. The quatrain stanza and iambic stress pattern prevail; of the twenty-seven rhymed poems in *Heart-Shape*, at least a dozen are structured with, or consist of two or three quatrain stanzas. However, when Hayden within that collection moves away from straightforward narrative or lyrical poetry, he also varies his prosody.

In the "voice" pieces such as "Ole Jim Crow," "Shine, Mister?,"
and "Bacchanale," he accommodates the spoken vernacular with
appropriate abbreviation and variation in line and stanza lengths,
using rhyme for repetition and rhetorical stress, or not at all.

These and other early poems imitative of spoken or sung "folk
language" may be imitative also of Sterling Brown, Langston
Hughes, and other contemporaries practicing the same techniques,
but Hayden in these instances progresses toward his own unique
voice as he consciously experiments with the formal aspects of his
work. By *The Lion and the Archer* he has forsaken rhyme for the
sake of rhyme; he has objectified his imagery, seeking a concrete
sensuousness more conducive to symbolic reinforcement of theme;
and he has begun to let stanzas determine their own lengths according to the logical and dramatic development of specific subject
matters.

Perhaps the chief feature of Hayden's early technical development is his pursuit of dramatic quality in his poetry. He manifests
this impulse frequently in varied formats of interior monologue,
dramatic dialogue, or in montages of mixed narrative voices that
have thematic unity. The early examples suggest the tendency more
than they portend the subsequent refinement, but his practice in
this mode begins as early as his earliest published works and recurs
with increasing frequency and enhanced quality as his poetic
knowledge and skill develop. In brief, Hayden's poetry after *Heart-
Shape* begins to show the conscious effort to refine his craft, as he
expands his subject matters, and tries new methods for expressing
them. Some of the results are evident in *The Lion and the Archer*.
He published previously and separately other equally compelling
"proofs" during the early 1940s, later collecting and publishing
them together with more recent work completed during the next
decade. Following this progression through scrutiny of those poems
initially printed or reprinted in those collections, *Figure of Time*
(1955), *A Ballad of Remembrance* (1962), and *Selected Poems*
(1966), reveals the extent and direction of Hayden's continuous
growth through his "midcareer" period.

## Chapter Three
# Poems in the Passage Time I: Personals and People
## Chartings of Continuity

Because *A Ballad of Remembrance* (1962) was a long time coming, it incorporates work that shows developmental trends from Robert Hayden's early experience to his then most recent innovations. Some of the poems with origins in the 1930s had appeared in print as early as the mid-1940s; some derive from Hayden's travel experience, and memories of his personal history recorded in the 1950s; and a few poems reflect the Baha'i religious themes he first directly addressed in *Figure of Time* (1955). Twenty-two of the thirty-six poems in *A Ballad* appear in print for the first time in that inaugural volume in Paul Breman's Heritage Series. Following the Dakar Grand Prize and favorable American reviews in belated response to *A Ballad* in 1965, Hayden selected and revised *Ballad* poems and then added thirteen new poems to form *Selected Poems* for New York publication in 1966. Thus the work in these two substantial collections spans the crucial decades in Hayden's midcareer. *A Ballad of Remembrance* and *Selected Poems* together represent a sustained period of productivity, and the poems therein trace Hayden's passage from explorer to seeker to finder of his personal poetic *Zeitgeist*.

### Personals

The personal poems in these two collections reflect a significant trend in Hayden's artistic method of dealing with inner agony and bittersweet memories. Although he ''withheld'' his personal voice in *The Lion and the Archer* and subdued it in *Figure of Time*, a tightly controlled articulation of accumulated feeling finds its way into *A Ballad* and *Selected Poems*. However, in both volumes

Hayden seeks indirection and finds artistic modes with which to "exteriorize" these emotion-charged lyrics. "The Web" (*BR*, 31; *SP*, 56) and "The Wheel" (*BR*, 33; *SP*, 57) especially exemplify this midcareer effort to allegorize feelings of inadequacy, insecurity, guilt, and recrimination. In spite of speaking in the first person in these two poems, Hayden uses concrete symbolism and analogy to carry their similar messages. For example, the speaker of "The Web" accidentally tears a spider's web; that event triggers "embittered thoughts" that equate his own condition with being ensnared in a similar, yet "more intricate," web.

Hayden considerably improves the poem through revision, and the version in *Selected Poems* more nearly correlates form and meaning. There he augments the original claim that his psychic web is paradoxically fragile and indestructible by reducing his format to wispy three-line stanzas of only three or four words per line, devoid of the many polysyllabics in the *Ballad* version. Thus, on the page, the poem in appearance resembles the "iron gossamer" from which escape is impossible. Also, in stressing that the tearing of the "real" web was no more than a chance event, he heightens the dramatic tension between acknowledgment of a seemingly inevitable condition and the dark introspection of that status as occurring only by chance. While the poem seems a lament, an expression of resigned defeat, both its ostensibly accidental occasion and its symbolic center suggest a chronic yet sporadic form of emotional agony. Similarly, "The Wheel" comprises a concrete, quasi-allegorical image (a circular torture rack), which by its very nature rotates recurrently but which thereby also suggests temporary relief from emotional distress that is tortuous but neither continuous nor debilitating.

Because "The Web" and "The Wheel" express feelings that recur, one cannot simply associate a biographical time frame with these personal poems. Other personals in these two collections, however, more clearly derive from Hayden's adult recollections of his youth. These poems he collectively designated "memory poems." He wrote some of them during the 1950s when he attained detachment through a fortuitous combination of elapsed time and deliberate technique. No doubt that midlife identity crisis, when in 1953 he discovered that he was never legally adopted, caused him to think back again to his early days and his parents. He later said he had then a need to recall his past in order to purge himself of some of its pain.[1]

One such poem, while classified a personal poem by Hayden, could well be regarded a place poem or a heritage poem, since " 'Summertime and the Living . . .' " (*FT*, 2–3; *BR*, 26–27; *SP*, 53) describes much the same milieu as the earlier "Sunflowers: Beaubien Street." Of course, the difference is that Hayden puts his younger self in "Summertime," albeit in the guise of a third person, obliquely included rather than clearly identified or characterized. As he has pointed out, he was looking at himself in a different time dimension, and so the "external" persona represents his memory of his earlier self in that prior cultural and emotional context.[2] As in "Sunflowers" he captures the ambience of folk culture, but to "Summertime" he adds personal recollections of his "elders" and his present ambivalent attitude toward them.

He sustains this attitudinal approach through an objective balance, based on contrasts between fantasy and reality, between nostalgic reverie and distressful recollection of harsh and troubled lives. The increasingly skillful poet of *Selected Poems* tightens the poem's structure and thus enhances the dramatic coherence of "Summertime" by altering it from six short stanzas of arbitrary lengths in *Figure* and *Ballad* to the four eight-line verse paragraphs of the "final" version.

Hayden's narrator begins the poem by reporting that "nobody planted roses" in the slums and goes on to contrast the absence of roses with the abundant, symbolic sunflowers, which, like the people, are "tough-stalked and bold," and, like ghetto children, are "vivid" and "unplanned." In following his basic organizational technique, a reverie motif based on the logic of free association, Hayden then shifts from the general to the specific, from children to himself as a child. He recalls in third person his own childhood forms of fantasy as escapes from the harshness of home life:

> There circus-poster horses curveted
> in trees of heaven
> above the quarrels and shattered glass,
> and he was bareback rider of them all.

Retrospectively, the speaker attributes adult hostility to adult frustration, as he re-creates ghetto summer activities in terms of denial and deprivation. With "no roses . . . except when people died," and no summer vacations, the "elders" even during "the

poor folks' time'' were limited in their leisure to ''wafting hearsay
with funeral-parlor fans / or making evening solemn by / their
quietness.'' He concludes the third stanza with another personal
application, as one who still feels on him the ''Mosaic eyes'' of those
morally upright elders, harshened by their lives, and harshening his
in return.

Hayden once more shifts from personal to general in concluding
the poem itself. From previous stanzas he extends the contrasts between the freedom of youthful fantasy and the grim reality of adult
limitations and expands this dichotomy into a street scene
dominated by the conjunction of joyless virtue and ''tolerant
wickednesss.'' The poet's description of ''grim street preachers''
shaking tambourines (for lucre) and Bibles (for show) ''in the face /
of tolerant wickedness'' brings the reverie to a close with his mature
adult perspective, cognizant of hypocrisy, and appreciative of the
humane aspects of ''immoral'' lives. Once on the street, Hayden's
''memory picture'' includes also the community events he
associates with those streets. He chooses ''Elks parades and big
splendiferous / Jack Johnson in his diamond limousine'' as
examples to suggest the then current sources of collective pride and
hope. With the particular image of Jack Johnson, Hayden
summarizes the balanced strategy of the poem: Johnson
symbolically epitomizes both the ''hurt'' and the ''glory'' of
Hayden's youth and of his race during his youth. Johnson's glory
days ended with his racial persecution, just as the future glory of
Ethiopia's god-fearing race remained yet unfulfilled at the time of
Hayden's poetic reverie.

The poet subsequently attributed his achievement of an
objectivity in his later personal poems to the very process of writing
such poems as ''Summertime.''[3] There seems no reason to question
the validity of that attribution since ''Summertime'' itself in its
content, structure, and narrative perspective bespeaks just such a
progression, an artful balancing of fact and fantasy, technique and
sentiment.

Through similar striving for, and achievement of, objective indirection, Hayden memorializes both of his foster parents in *A
Ballad* and *Selected Poems*. In two instances he uses similar
''memory'' modes of self-inclusion; in two other poems he retells
the life stories of each parent through fictional mini-biographies
with more dramatic interest than direct autobiographical revela-

tion. In perhaps his most frequently anthologized and most widely read poems, Hayden recalls William Hayden with "Those Winter Sundays," and Sue Westerfield Hayden with "The Whipping." The universal appeal of these two memory pieces attests to Hayden's detached artistry in dealing with painful experiences; scrutiny of his method convinces one that the appeal is as aesthetic as it is emotional.

## Personals—"Memory Poems"

"Those Winter Sundays" (*BR*, 29; *SP*, 55) comes close to perfection in expressing sentiment without being sentimental. Hayden, the first-person speaker, pays warm tribute to his foster father by acknowledging belatedly the father's love that Robert as a callow youth could not appreciate at the time. This contrast of retrospective warmth and remembered cold indifference reviews accurately Hayden's present and past emotional stances. In fact, he uses "real" and figurative temperature contrasts to maintain artistic control of the lyric. One can discern three distinct levels of such "temperature control"—physical, figurative or emotional, and tonal—all of which interact to make "Sundays" a "cool" poem in the familiar Wordsworthian sense of "emotion recollected in tranquility."

On the descriptive physical level the poem literally heats up as it progresses. The Sunday-morning household temperature goes from "blueblack cold" in the first stanza to a "splintering, breaking" of that cold, producing warm rooms early in the second stanza. From the outset the speaker identifies his father as the source of warmth, who "made / banked fires blaze," and "who had driven out the cold." Interestingly, Hayden for *Selected Poems* deleted the line "and smell the iron and velvet bloom of heat" from his initial *Ballad* version, possibly because he realized the olfactory imagery would diffuse the concentration on temperature as an indicator of emotional response. In any event, the speaker acknowledges that as a boy he responded to this physical warmth with cold ingratitude. He recalls "speaking indifferently to him" and remembers that "no one ever thanked him."

The second level of temperature contrasts includes not only the emotional atmosphere of cold apathy, but also a partial rationale for young Hayden's coolness toward his parent. The boy welcomes the physical warmth his father provides on a cold winter morning, but he lingers in bed because he fears the heated arguments of his family, "the chronic angers of that house." Ironically, as the physical temperature rises in the home, so does the level of emotional stress. Temperature variation thus connotes both unappreciated paternal love as an "austere office" and the boy's anxiety in dread of the mutual hostility of frustrated parents.

The third level cannot be quoted into focus because it resides within the intangible effect of the overall authorial tone of the poem. Hayden's tribute in gratitude ends in the implicit balance of its climactic rhetorical question. He puts a realistic "cold edge" on the nostalgic warmth of his poem by concluding on a note of regret, chiding himself for failures now beyond redemption: "What did I know, what did I know / of love's austere and lonely offices?" Through the restraint of careful craftsmanship, Hayden infuses "Those Winter Sundays" with timeless truth about parent-child relationships, thereby providing a basis for reader response that is vicariously prompted yet aesthetically justified.

The crafted remembrance of his foster mother, "The Whipping" (BR, 28; SP, 45), also reviews childhood anxiety, again recalled with an adult's compassion for its parental sources. Here Hayden employs a combination of alternating narrative perspectives and spatial movement within the narrative to relate physical event and emotional response. He divides the content, six four-line stanzas of free verse, into three distinct narrative sections, marked off by shifts from third-person narration to the first person and then back again to a third-person conclusion. Through this device, Hayden traces the mode of memory whereby he recalls a past event from the "outside," then subjectively relives the intense emotion of that moment, and finally moves outward again to an adult understanding of the event and its emotional causes and effects.

In straightforward narrative description the poet relates the recurrent punishment he experienced as a child:

> The old woman across the way
> is whipping the boy again
> and shouting to the neighborhood
> her goodness and his wrongs.

The external perspective of the scene, viewed ''across the way,'' continues on a spatial basis in subsequent stanzas, as the old woman chases the boy around the yard while he ''crashes through elephant ears, / pleads in dusty zinnias.'' Through the first four stanzas Hayden depicts the event as it might be viewed by neighbors. But recollection of the physical punishment (''She strikes and strikes the shrilly circling / boy till the stick breaks in her hand'') prompts also the author's recall of accompanying verbal abuse and emotional devastation.

Significantly, he calls these recollections ''woundlike memories,'' as he shifts the narration to first person. Hayden relives that moment of torment in the terms of its most traumatic effect:

> My head gripped in bony vise
> of knees, the writhing struggle
> to wrench free, the blows, the fear
> worse than blows that hateful
> Words could bring, the face that I
> no longer knew or loved . . .

While the poet sharply conveys the physical intensity of the event with the vivid tactile imagery of ''head gripped in bony vise / of knees,'' his emphasis is on the psychological wounds, an emphasis he subtly reinforces through the irony of seeking womblike protection from maternal abuse by assuming the fetal position.

Hayden brings the painful reverie to a close by reverting to the external third-person perspective. He shifts attention from ''the boy,'' whom he strategically relocates to leave him sobbing in his room, to ''the woman,'' still outside in the yard, leaning ''muttering against a tree.'' Having by them purged himself of ''woundlike memories,'' the mature poet better understood that the physical and mental abuse dealt out by his foster mother derived at least partially from her own physical condition and emotional pain.[4] His whipping left her ''exhausted, purged— / avenged in part for lifelong hidings / she has had to bear.'' In the light of the final perspective, Hayden's conclusion completes his own purgation and casts the subject in an empathetic tone. Yet ''The Whipping'' as a childhood reverie ''outgrows'' its occasion, subject, and strictly biographical category. Because Hayden exorcises his personal demons with careful control of narrative technique, his poem, both in subject and theme, applies and thus appeals widely to all who took their own lickings "then" and who now recognize the psychological concomitants of childhood punishments. Indeed, the ultimate appeal of Hayden's "personal" poem may be its instructive effect in helping readers put their own "woundlike memories" in better perspective. Such a possibility testifies to the validity of Hayden's artistic credo—to enrich general human experience through poetic translation of its particulars.

## Personals—Family Portraits

If Sue Hayden is the subject of "The Whipping," she is the object of "The Ballad of Sue Ellen Westerfield" (*SP*, 21–22), a personal poem only in the sense that Hayden uses her maiden name, and selected aspects of her biography and personality, as materials for dramatic fiction. As one might expect from his title, the poet in "The Ballad" narrates a story, dramatizes a life, and enlivens a character. In so doing he treats the theme of interracial love for dramatic effect rather than protest purpose. Commensurate with his conception of history, his view of the past as an integral part of the present, Hayden sets the story of Sue Ellen in the past, while portraying her person in the present. She thereby becomes a vivid product, if not the captive, of her past.

This time merger reaches backward and forward from a central dramatic event. Hayden introduces Sue Westerfield as the mulatto daughter of a mother freed by her owner, Sue Ellen's father, and characterizes her largely on the basis of a single trait. "She hardened in perilous rivertowns" during the Civil War, and afterwards disdained male attention while working as a maid on a Mississippi riverboat. Her beauty attracted that attention, but her pride refused it: "Rivermen reviled her for the rankling cold / sardonic pride / that gave a knife-edge to her comeliness." Hayden establishes this trait with an expository first stanza and then flashes forward to Sue Ellen's old age to present her story as her recollections, cast in terse poetic narrative, in her mind's eye, but not in her language. That story includes dramatic action (fire aboard the riverboat, with its dangers, heroics, and survival), plot (interracial, lost love), and theme (the cruelty of human circumstance). Hayden uses repetition (anaphora primarily), along with functional variety ("crazing

horrors,'' ''swifting flames,'' ''savaging panic'') and compounding
(''flamelit,'' ''hellmouth''), to render vividly the fire and its
aftermath. But he leads up to and from that dramatic event with a
cryptic account of the love story, emphasizing its difficulty and her
pride.

Although Sue Ellen's ''sardonic pride'' seems in abeyance with
her white lover's ''voice quickening her,'' even as she fell in love she
''cursed the circumstance.'' Their love cannot stand the light of
society's day, but in the fire-illuminated night Sue Ellen and her
lover find each other and escape both the flames and social
constraint:

> How long how long was it they wandered,
> loving fearing loving,
> fugitives whose dangerous only hidingplace
> was love?

Eventually, inevitably, the lovers part, not because of social pressure or interference, but because Sue Ellen ''could not forfeit
what she was, / even for him—could not, even for him, / forswear
her pride.'' Hayden punctuates their separation through historical
parallelism, closing the poem with a frame structure which again
merges past and present. Just as Sue Ellen's white father tearfully
freed and lost her mother, so her white lover at their parting ''wept
as had her father once.'' But the tragedy is hers. She retains in old
age both her pride (''her back still straight'') and her sardonic bit-
terness: ''Until her dying-bed, / she cursed the circumstance.''

Thus Hayden with the raw materials of his foster mother's life
constructs a dramatic ballad with independent thematic interest.
Although Jim Barlow, Sue Hayden's dead first husband, held an
overlong claim on her emotional allegiance, and although this claim
mitigated her devotion to Hayden's foster father, that ''lost love''
was neither interracial nor as glamorous as its fictional counterpart.[5]
Perhaps as one of those ''wearisome kith and kin'' whom Sue
Westerfield Hayden neglected by living in her bittersweet past,
Robert Hayden simply followed a compensatory impulse in creating
''The Ballad,'' subconsciously romanticizing his mother's past to
rationalize its attraction for her, and thus rationalizing as well her
emotional neglect of him and his father. More probably, as an accomplished artist Hayden retrospectively saw in his foster mother
another proof of the abundant and often cruel ironies of life, and by

then had "distanced" himself sufficiently to write her story.[6] By taking poetic license with the facts, he could pay belated tribute to the real person and in the process create another character and a poem notable for its qualities independent of biographical sources, a "true" ballad in the strictest sense of that generic classification.

His father's story, "The Burly Fading One" (*FT*, 8; *BR*, 16; *SP*, 45), is shorter than "The Ballad," and only as tenuously related to actual biography. He converts William Hayden to "Uncle Jed," to the status of a deceased relative seen only vaguely in a fading tintype photograph, and recalled only briefly in terms of occupations, personal traits, and the remembrance of innuendo by petty-minded relatives. If this mode of "distancing" seems more drastic than that of Sue Hayden's "Ballad," one can note that "The Burly Fading One" considerably predates "Ballad" both in year of composition and in degree of authorial growth. For example, in his revision for *Selected Poems*, Hayden deletes some of the fiction (Uncle Jed is still a railroad man, but no longer widely traveled and worldly) and retains all of the fact (Uncle Jed, like William Hayden, is still a religiously devout teetotaler). The two primary aspects of the portrait, Jed's love of life and the enmity he incurred among wife and relatives, seem exaggerated but authentic in real source. Hayden thus accurately reflects personal traits to commemorate his foster father and adds adventure and conflict to create dramatic interest. Uncle Jed, the "bullyboy / of wintered recollections," brawls and loves his way through life as "coal miner, stevedore and railroad man" and dies violently in the Johnstown flood trying "to save the jolly girl / his wife had mortally wished dead," or "so sibling innuendos all aver." As Hayden's own memory of his father fades with time, he sharpens that image for himself and provides his reader a drama in miniature. It is a life only implicitly dramatized, a personage only fleetingly glimpsed. Like Hayden's objective correlative, the poem is a fading photograph that intrigues rather than informs, a picture that evokes both his memory and the reader's imagination.

## Personals—Introspective Poems

"The Diver" (*SP*, 11–12), the lead poem in *Selected Poems*, exemplifies the midcareer mastery of Hayden's artfully disguised expressions of personal introspection that probe inward rather than reach backward. As symbolically indirect as the earlier "The Web" and "The Wheel," "The Diver" exhibits a notable refinement in subtle analogy. In an allegorical descent into the subconscious, Hayden likens a dark night of his soul to an exploratory dive to the ocean's floor by a scuba diver. Shaping the poem subtly but deliberately with abbreviated line lengths to suggest the columnar path of a diver's descent, with its trail of rising air bubbles, the poet "conceals" his own psyche behind the mask of the anonymous diver.[7]

The poem reads coherently and quite effectively as no more than a vividly descriptive account of a diver experiencing "the rapture of the deep," whether physiologically induced nitrogen narcosis or a brief infatuation with submerged suicidal tendencies. Hayden, however, presents this journey through "infraspace" with narrative mode and irony of description that provoke a parallel psychological interpretation as well. The diver, describing what he observes during the descent, remains curiously passive and somehow "removed" for a considerable portion of this description. Not until he reaches the bottom, and the ruin of a sunken ship, does he literally locate himself in the narrative ("I entered / the wreck"). Prior references to his movement came without the subjective, phrased as contrasts between his inactive descent and the furious pace observed among the flora and fauna of his pelagic medium. While the diver "sank," "descended," "freefalling, weightless," other organisms "flashed and / shimmered," "swarmed," "prised," and "thronged."

Ironic contrasts continue in the description of "the dead ship, / [the] carcass that swarmed with / voracious life." Inside the ship, the diver encounters another form of "life": inanimate objects given movement and vitality through the dual prisms of the speaker's murky visual perspective and his ironic mental acuity. He reports seeing "the sad slow / dance of gilded / chairs, the ectoplasmic / swirl of garments, / drowned instruments / of bouyancy, / drunken shoes." But psychological projections quickly supplant these surrealistic physical apparitions in the speaker's imagination, as he "sees" also "livid gesturings, / eldritch hide and / seek of laughing / faces." Ironically, while his response to these visions is emotional rather than physical, he uses intense, physically active verbs to convey his yearning. He wishes "to / find," "to fling," "to call," "to yield." Hayden succinctly characterizes this paradoxical condition of psychologically active stasis by using oxymorons to describe his diver in a dreamlike state of "languid / frenzy."

The sirenlike temptations remain mysterious in identity, yet clear enough in the nature of their allure. "Those hidden ones" beckon the speaker with "livid gesturings," "laughing / faces," "rapturous / whisperings," "cancelling arms," and "numbing kisses." The diver resists these sensual appeals only with great difficulty. He later ponders the stimulus of his survival: was it a "Reflex of life-wish?" or the "Respirator's brittle / belling?" that called him back from the brink? The question remains open as he recounts his ascent in similar uncertain terms: "Swam from / the ship somehow; / somehow began the / measured rise."

As graphically realistic as "The Diver" is in depicting the beauty and risks of deepsea diving, the poem presents in symbolic synopsis a deeply personal emotional crisis as well. Hayden's diver plumbs the depths of his creator's psyche, measuring the strength of the poet's desire to break through the bonds of social and moral restraint in pursuit of potentially self-destructive pleasures. Hayden thus personally embodies, and artistically portrays, the classic struggle between the Freudian id and superego. The diver's yearning to "have / done with self and / every dinning / vain complexity" represents more than narcosis, more than even a death-wished-for release from emotional perturbation. It suggests a strong urge to forsake all external considerations, to forego "respectability," to expend the id in more than dreams, in a public milieu rather than just in private thoughts. The impulse to "unmask," to disregard the concerns of identity, conformity, and concealment, at once epitomizes the strength and danger of that urge.

The speaker's interior query about his survival does not demystify the process for him, but with it Hayden clarifies the workings of his own superego. When the diver wonders if he managed to resist the call of the deep because of an instinctive "life-wish," or because of the "brittle / belling" of the air-supply warning advice, Hayden ponders whether his adherence to social conformity can be attributed to an instinctive pain-avoidance response, or to the externally imposed "belling" of learned social and moral restraints. In doing so, he acknowledges a state of accommodation, with the "reality principle" of his ego back in control. Completely consistent with his allegorical premise, the poet only begins his "measured rise"; he neither obviates another descent nor removes his analogical mask entirely. In thus depicting his own dark dreams, Hayden produces a multi-layered statement about the human psyche, a laminated work of art with its foundations in archetypal and psychological footings, but with its roots in his own emotional experience.

A final personal poem representative of Hayden's mid-career has its antecedents in the experience of a specific event. As such, "Electrical Storm" (*SP*, 13–14) is an occasional narrative bracketed within a personal context. One night in the early 1960s when Hayden and Erma returned home from the Fisk University campus through a summer storm, they were warned by their neighbors, Arna and Alberta Bontemps, who shouted across the street to the Haydens, telling them not to step out of their car because a downed "live" power line was laying across their yard. This narrow escape prompted Hayden in the months thereafter to contemplate the vagaries of life, within the framework of his past and present interpretations of natural forces, human vulnerability, and mortal destiny. "Electrical Storm" is the result, a philosophical yet highly personal re-creation of that experience.

In the poem, Hayden establishes a narrative basis for this contemplation by recalling from his youth the inherent paradoxes of folk-cultural religious beliefs and superstitious notions. He reports somewhat disparagingly his elders' attribution of lightning and thunder in their folk-language references to an Old Testament angry God's displeasure with sinful mortals ("He don't like ugly."). The narrator merges in the initial stanza the elders' fundamentalist formulae with their secular superstitions about mysteries beyond their comprehension, such as their belief that windows and dogs somehow attracted lightning. Hayden thus portrays "the grey neglected ones" of his youth as they "huddled under Jehovah's oldtime wrath," paradoxically both "trusting, [and] afraid." In the second stanza the poet personalizes the account by tracing his own progression from ignorant, guilt-induced fear ("I huddled too, when a boy, / mindful of things they'd told me / God was bound to make me answer for") to an educated understanding of meteorological phenomena ("pressure systems, / colliding massive energies / that make a storm"). Yet those former cultural influences remain, included implicitly in

Hayden's language. Even as he recalls being "colleged," exchanging superstition for knowledge, his elders' advice echoes through the narrative: "Beware the infidels, my son."

Hayden directly applies that background to the immediate occasion by introducing his storm narrative with the transitional phrase "Well for us . . .". In a vivid synopsis, highlighted by the "special effects" of unique modifiers and verbals, the poet briefly describes the electrical storm:

> Last night we drove
> through suddenly warring weather.
> Wind and lightning havocked,
> berserked in wires, trees.

Emphasizing the storm's effect while suspending the earlier questions of cause, Hayden includes pointed detail that deftly foreshadows the subsequent philosophical balance of mystery and certainty. The unknown danger awaiting the Haydens ("Fallen lines we could not see at first") becomes metaphysically significant as a symbol of the risks of an inordinate faith in secular knowledge. He pairs in narrative context and in immediate spatial proximity the fallen lines carrying man-made electricity with another effect of the storm: "The hedge was burning in the rain." By evoking through allusion the burning bush of the Old Testament, Hayden reiterates the tension between, and hints at a reconciliatory balancing of, "old time religion" and secular knowledge.

"Electrical Storm" concludes on that note but goes well beyond a simple balance of religion and science in the poet's speculation about the mystery of human beings' vulnerability and their particular survival:

> Who knows if it was heavenly design
> or chance
> (or knows if there's a difference, after all)
> that brought us and our neighbors through—
> though others died—
> the archetypal dangers of the night?

Finally, the speaker closes the circle of narrative perspective with another reference to his elders, reminding himself of their answers to such questions: "I know what those / cowering true believers would have said.'' While he no longer can accept their oversimple view that storms are personally directed warnings to sinners, neither can he discount the possibly spiritual origin of inexplicable "chance." After rejecting the guilt imposed by his fundamentalist upbringing, Hayden sought and found an alternate spiritual perspective. But the electrical storm reminds him that life is ultimately mysterious. In this realization he cannot sustain contempt for the elders' superstitious response to that mystery. So his final reference to "cowering true believers" implies an emphathetic view of those with whom he shares an ignorance differing in kind, but perhaps not in ultimate degree. The central irony of the poem, and the quality that makes it most personal, is that when Hayden contemplates his own limits of understanding, he achieves an enhanced appreciation for similar limits among his forebears and, implicitly, among mankind in general.

The poet enforces the metaphysical catechism of "Electrical Storm" with subtle shifts in tone. For example, he sketches his personal progression from ignorant guilt and fear, to false intellectual certainty, to enlightened but humble "ignorance." Simultaneously, he shifts his treatment of those "grey neglected ones" from almost sardonic disdain to sympathetic understanding. Hayden leavens both of these transitions with self-deprecatory wry humor that originates in his use of folk language and verbal irony. According to Hayden, "Electrical Storm" was "one of my most personal poems."[8] Yet the poem transcends its immediate occasion and biographical antecedents because the poet probes a mystery as old as the sphinx and as timely as the present. In its transcendent pursuit of hidden truth, this particular poem shares thematic similarity with many of Hayden's personal poems and, indeed, with much of his mature work of whatever critically convenient category.

## People

Hayden's personal portraits of his foster father and mother reveal much about his memories of those real people and indicate perhaps as much about his interest in character portrayal regardless of its source. Several portrait poems in *A Ballad of Remembrance* and *Selected Poems* reflect this interest and illustrate the poet's evolving skill in this subgenre. As in previous practice, some of these profiles derive from real sources, either particular individuals or as composites. Others are entirely imaginary—fictional characters based on psychological fact.

One such persona, introduced in *Figure of Time* and reprinted in the later collections, illustrates the fictional category and suggests Hayden's developing propensity for dramatic or interior monologue. "Incense of the Lucky Virgin" (*FT*, 9; *BR*, 17; *SP*, 46), through the voice of a deranged victim of circumstance, dramatizes the source and result of the female persona's condition. Rather like the speaker in Robert Browning's "Porphyria's Lover," Hayden's speaker unknowingly reveals the extent of her derangement through her rambling monologue.

Desperate to provide for her three children after being deserted by her husband, she turned to conjure in the forms of "Incense of the Lucky Virgin" and "High John the Conqueror," supposedly magical potions and roots, the former a brand name devised by the poet for "created" irony, the latter a real brand name used for its authenticity and contextual irony. These folk "cures" prove futile—they "didn't bring him home again, / didn't get his children fed." Similarly useless are prayers and candlelight vigils. The speaker expresses her despair and unwittingly foreshadows its tragic consequences in her refrain, "An evening came I prayed no more / and blew my candles out, / oh blew my candles out." Hayden emphasizes her efforts as repeated ritual with the chantlike repetition of the final lines of the first two stanzas.

The perspective and level of activity alter in the third stanza. The incoherent woman repeats her prior directions to her children, in effect reliving the experience by again telling them to put on their Sunday best and to shine their shoes. She also recalls the children's responses, mixtures of happiness and curiosity. In the final stanza Hayden abruptly reveals the magnitude of this personal tragedy through the woman's disjointed but crazily calm revelation of her children's fates:

> Garland was too quick for me
> (he didn't yell once as he ran);
> Cleola, Willie Mae
> won't be hungry any more,
>     oh they'll never cry and hunger any more.

Upon realizing that deprivation and despair have driven the speaker to murder her own children, the reader better understands the poem's inherent ironies. The failure of hope, whether in folk superstition or religious faith, becomes doubly ironic as the despairing woman dresses her children in their Sunday clothes in preparation for death. Moreover, that she can find no solace in the "Incense of the Lucky Virgin" reminds us that she is a terribly unlucky nonvirgin; as the victim of her female vulnerability she cannot escape like her husband did and her young son does. Neither can the omnipotent male folk-hero figure of "High John the Conqueror" relieve her plight. Seemingly, only the obedient, resigned females die passively or go crazy in despair.

One may be initially tempted to reshape Hayden's psychological profile into a protest poem, citing the oppressive social causes of such tragedy, and then applying such a reading to a racial lament. Such a critical impulse, however, cannot be sustained. While certainly the folk elements of conjure and the stereotypical names of the children suggest a black identity in the poem, the woman's response to her plight seems too peculiarly bizarre for a valid protest application. Also her identity seems embedded in a larger archetypal consciousness, akin to the origins of the Medea myth, of which the subject-speaker of this monologue seems a modern manifestation. There can be no doubt that Hayden portrays the woman as both a helpless victim and a helpless perpetrator of social evil, but he seems more intent on psychological drama than on polemic purpose. In the poet's words about the poem, "It has nothing to do with race, although she's more likely to be thought of—I suppose—as an Afro-American woman. But no point is made about race. It's simply a folk poem."[9]

In another portrait poem, also a "folk poem" in which "no point is made about race," Hayden through elaborate detail and baroque diction brings to life in all his cultural and personal complexity a character he designates simply "Witch Doctor" (*BR*, 18–22; *SP*, 47–49). No "grim street preacher," this character seems more akin to the flamboyant, inspiring showman of Hayden's recollected vision of Jack Johnson.[10] The poet treats his subject as a psychologically complex individual and an intriguing cultural phenomenon. With extensive, functional application of baroque diction, Hayden conveys the character's subconscious motivation, his colorful external appearance, and his flamboyant public performance.

By restructuring the revised version, Hayden clearly distinguishes these perspectives. In the first three sections of approximately equal lengths, the poet presents respectively the witch doctor's private "life style," his mother's on-site preparations for his evening appearance, and his chauffeured travel from private indulgence to public performance. Significantly, the preacher, whose appeal is emotional, physical, and summed up in the phrase "outrageous flair," virtually never speaks throughout the length of the poem, notably including the long section descriptive of his "sermon." We do hear his mother, his "priestess in gold lamé," warming up the audience as "she prepares the way for mystery / and lucre." In folk language associated with street preachers more "conventional" than her son, she exhorts the audience by praising his powers. He is

> God's dictaphone of all-redeeming truth.
> Oh he's the holyweight champeen who's come
> to give the knockout lick to your bad luck;
> say he's the holyweight champeen who's here
> to deal a knockout punch to your hard luck.

Such "familiar" jargon prepares through contrast for the witch doctor's performance, which itself is all emotion and gesture, devoid of articulation, except for an opening mock prayer. Thereafter, with "mask in place" and device at hand,

> he sways, quivers, gesticulates as if
> to ward off blows or kisses, and when he speaks
> again he utters wildering vocables,
> hypnotic no-words planned (and never failing)
> to enmesh his flock in theopathic tension.

Hayden describes this "glittering flourish" with language designed to dazzle, to parallel verbally the orgiastic emotional indulgence thereby depicted. A cataloging of such "excessive" diction loses little even when out of context: "sinquecento, cynosure, quondam, allegros, surpliced, chatoyant, theopathic, endaemonic, antiphons, glissando, ensorcelled." Although his "baroque style" by then had given way to more austere modes, the poet here employs such language not as "hyper-erudition" to show off his vocabulary, but to emphasize the witch doctor's deceptive artistry in confusing "show" and substance.

Even if the poem did no more than describe the methods and appeal of such a skillful charlatan, it would still be an effective character sketch. But Hayden's ultimate interest, as with the speaker of "Incense," is in the psychology of the character portrayed. The witch doctor, who so cleverly and consciously deceives his audience for profit, reaps also an emotional reward that culminates in self-deception. The reader can discern this element of the profile by "tracking" the private habits and narrative revelations of this fascinating, almost androgynous individual. Clearly, his adopted role has ended, if not begun, in self-worship. The first sentence of the poem shows the witch doctor in the solitary narcissism of a mirrored room: "He dines alone surrounded by reflections / of himself." In spite of, or more accurately because of, his power over his "flock," he deludes himself, along with them. In the closing lines of the poem Hayden clearly renders that syndrome:

> he dances, dances, ensorcelled and aloof,
> the fervid juba of God as lover, healer,
> conjurer. And of himself as God.

Because of the audience's need and his skill, the witch doctor fulfills for them fantasized roles that are sexual, physical, and spiritual. And, as a god of his own making, he dances in fulfillment of his own unconscious needs of similar nature. It is "the moment / his followers all day have hungered for, / but which is his alone." Ironically, the charlatan deceives his followers to accommodate his own deception; in so doing he artificially self-satisfies the same needs he exploits in them. As he "feels them yearn toward him / as toward a lover," he "exults before the image / of himself their trust gives back." The poem thus suggests an ultimate communion of self-deceivers. Beyond providing an iridescent display of poetic skill in portraying human psychology and cultural phenomena, Hayden implies a perverse redemptive value in even this most hollow sham. Again, his organic blending of form and function can scarcely be discerned, but it should not be ignored. "Witch Doctor" certainly deserves more critical scrutiny and less oversimple disparagement than it has thus far prompted.[11]

Hayden also patterned another portrait after a "religious performer" in the person of Lula Butler Hurst, a popular gospel singer during Hayden's earlier years in Detroit. He entitles the poem

"Mourning Poem for the Queen of Sunday" (*BR*, 23; *SP*, 50), as an
apparently straightforward indication of his purpose and her
character. But with Hayden nothing is ever that simple, because his
acute awareness of life's ironies was complex, uncannily accurate, and
insatiable. The portrait of "Madame Butler" (as she was "billed")
incorporates his perception of the tension between appearance and
reality.

By using her wake as the poem's ostensible occasion, and by
creating an anonymous folk speaker to raise rhetorical questions expressive of group curiosity, the poet lends immediacy to the portrait. But the central drama derives from the tension between
Madame Butler's artistry in devoted service to God and Sunday audiences, and her violent death, compounded by its subtle implication of a sordid private life. Hayden even embeds these disparate
elements in the seemingly simple title. Butler in the eyes of her admirers was the "Queen of Sunday," but her brutal murder by her
lover arouses morbid curiosity about the other six days of the week.
The repeated refrain—"Who would have thought / she'd end that
way?"—connotes an element of self-righteousness in their
"mourning," especially when regarded in conjunction with the
repeated moral equation of sin and death: "Satan sweet-talked her,
/ four bullets hushed her."

This "mourning poem" then expresses not so much Hayden's
personal grief as his imagined characterization of the group
response to Butler's death. "They" lament their loss more than
they grieve her death because they had formerly drawn inspiration
from her performances. To them she represented divine "help with
struggling and doing without and being colored." Her Sunday
singing helped them make it through the week, but her violent
death reduces her to their level, forcing them to consider that she
too had to make it through. Not surprisingly, then, the speaker
evades that harsh truth in wistfully imagining that even the angels
mourn this "true believer" (at least "when she rared back her head
and sang"). The group spokesman also wishes that she could once
more "turn this quiet into shouting Sunday / and make folks forget
what she did on Monday."

As in his homage to Bessie Smith, Hayden designs this poem with
stanzaic breaks, language, rhythms, and tones suggestive of the
repertoire for which Butler was famed. Like a gospel song, "Mourning Poem" alternates narrative elaboration and choral refrain. In its

abbreviated line lengths and accentuation the refrain seems ready-made for hand clapping. The concluding stanza exemplifies these features:

> Oh, Satan sweet-talked her,
> and four bullets hushed her.
> Lord's lost Him His diva,
> His fancy warbler's gone.
> Who would have thought,
> who would have thought she'd end that way?

And in those final lines Hayden summarizes the portrait's primary theme—the ironic disparities between Butler's public performance and her private life, and between human nature's yearning to be inspired by the former, and yet titillated by speculation about the latter. In this regard "Mourning Poem" characterizes those "mourners" as certainly as it eulogizes its ostensible subject.

Several more poems could be discussed in this chapter, but since "Perseus" and "Lear Is Gay" appear in revised versions in subsequent collections, and since the portraits of Nat Turner, Harriet Tubman, and Frederick Douglass are more appropriately treated later in the next chapter as heritage poems, one can conclude by citing a few recurring characteristic features of theme and technique among the diversity of previous portrait poems. Virtually all portraits share a cultural medium and reflect an interest in psychological aspects of personality and behavior. In effect, Hayden uses his culture as the stage and the portraits as individualized actors in a drama designed to probe beneath surface realities. These poems, informed by an ironic perspective and strengthened with symbolic suggestion, extend well beyond mere characterization. Each can be considered a drama in miniature; all reveal Hayden's empathetic concern for human vulnerability and his transcendent vision of human experience.

## Chapter Four

# Poems in the Passage Time II: Places and Heritage

Two general subject categories of "locale" poems recur in both *A Ballad of Remembrance* and *Selected Poems*. Hayden includes in those collections four poems about the South and eight titles under the heading "An Inference of Mexico." While risking oversimplification, one can summarize Hayden's place poems about the South by noting the similar features of those he selected for reprinting. Although all four poems in *A Ballad* depend on connections among history, locale, and contemporary atmosphere, Hayden's choice of "Tour 5" and "A Road in Kentucky" for *Selected Poems* suggests a priority based on a preference for drama over description.

## Places—Southern Scenes

"Locus" (*FT*, 4–5; *BR*, 8) and "On Lookout Mountain" (*BR*, 10) emphasize the intrusion of the past into the present with almost opposite effect. Imagining the southern scenery of "Locus" in symbolic terms of its violent history, the poet extends past glories and cruelties into presently perceived "native" attitudes:

> Here the past, adored and unforgiven,
> its wrongs, denials, grievous loyalties
>     alive in hard averted eyes—
> the very structure of the bones; soul-scape;
> of warring shades whose guns are real.

Contrarily, "On Lookout Mountain" expands the visual perspective from that Civil War mountaintop battleground into a vision of past heroic sacrifice now trivialized by tourism. The speaker notes this disparity between historic significance and contemporary superficiality in merging imaginatively the characteristic activities of past soldiers and present tourists on this historic site:

I gaze through depths of fool's-gold morning,
think of the death-for-foothold inching climb
of those imagines. Impossibly
they clambered up the crackling mountainside,
and here where alpinists of Sunday
pick souvenirs and views, here once in clouds
was staged a monster jamboree
of daring choices, dubious victory.

Expectably, the poem concludes in disheartened disillusionment, expressed in sardonic tones:

Have done, o heart. Behold how beautiful
upon this mountain the gadget feet of trivia
shine. O hear the taxidermic eagle sing.

Perhaps Hayden later considered these two poems overly harsh in their implicit judgment of his "contemporaries," or too inclusive in that judgment. More likely his interest in individually dramatized characterization caused him to drop "Locus" and "On Lookout Mountain," yet retain "Tour 5" and "A Road in Kentucky" for *Selected Poems.*

Both of these "southern road" poems use locale as a means to an end, to sustain drama through character interaction in particular rather than general terms. Hayden said he took his title for "Tour 5" (*BR*, 9; *SP*, 41) from an oil-company guidebook designator for the highway route from Nashville to Jackson, Mississippi, because he wanted a flat, nondescript title to contrast ironically with the tense drama of the poem's content.[1] That drama derives from an automobile trip Hayden and a white friend took along the old Natchez Trace, originally an Indian trail later traveled by fugitive slaves. The Trace had been a notorious haven for renegades, thieves, and murderers who preyed upon its travelers and each other. Seemingly oblivious to this history, Hayden's "travelog" begins in glorious color imagery of "autumn hills / in blazonry of farewell scarlet / and recessional gold." But an encounter with a local gas-station attendant reminds Hayden that bigotry also is an element of this contemporary setting:

We stop a moment in a town
watched over by Confederate sentinels,
buy gas and ask directions of a rawboned man
whose eyes revile us as the enemy.

The poet-traveler realizes that "Shrill gorgon silence breathes behind" the man's "taut civility." This recognition alters drastically his subsequent view of the once-glorious landscape. The "ever-tautening air" appears "dark for us despite its Indian summer glow." Henceforth, even children appear "wordless and remote," as they wave to the passing travelers "from kindling porches." The concluding lines imagistically express how the speaker's view of natural surroundings has been "colored" by a single human attitude:

> And now the land is flat for miles,
> the landscape lush, metallic, flayed,
> its brightness harsh as bloodstained swords.

"A Road in Kentucky" (*FT*, 18; *BR*, 11; *SP*, 43) evokes a dramatic story as Hayden relates physical setting to the past travels of a particular fictional persona. He plays out the imagined story of "that ballad lady" and her dying former lover on the stage of this "real" road. Within this technique Hayden almost personifies the road, and the setting thus becomes an intrinsic element of the "playlet." Apparently guilt-stricken at the news of the fatal condition of the former lover she jilted, "that ballad lady went / to ease the lover whose life she broke." The scenic features of the "road she took" symbolically suggest the emotional difficulty of her pilgrimage:

> road all hackled through barberry fire,
> through cedar and alder and sumac and thorn.
> Red clay stained her flounces
>     and stones cut her shoes
> and the road twisted on to his loveless house

In a particularly effective image, Hayden foretells the lover's death in the detail that denotes the woman's arrival at her lover's farm, where "his cornfield [is] dying / in the scarecrow's arms." After his death she retraces her route "in the cawing light" on that same road, now darkened by her grief, a road "so dark and so dark in the briary light." So many of the details of the dramatized human relationship are only implicitly evoked that one must vicariously share the poet's imaginative response to locale and setting.

This necessity measures the unique success of "A Road" as mini-drama, and partially accounts for the author's inclusion of the poem in his *Selected Poems*.

## Places—Inferences of Mexico

The set of Mexico poems, the product of Hayden's Ford Foundation year (1954–55) in that locale, seems at first as various as the landscape and culture it describes.[2] One cannot be certain whether Hayden arranged the eight "surviving" poems in *Selected Poems* according to geographical coverage, in chronological order of composition, or by deliberate thematic design, but two generalizations can be validated by reading the poems in any order. First, because the poet wanted to express the spirit of Mexican culture, rather than just reproduce picturesque detail, the work shows his strong sense of history. He recurrently emphasizes his sense of how, in Mexico, the past is everywhere dramatically tangible in the present. Second, and typically, Hayden's fascination with humanity, beyond fact or artifact, causes many of his Mexican scenes to be filled with living presences, ghosts of the past and contemporary "natives" affected by the impact of their cultural history.

For example, "An Inference of Mexico" opens with "Day of the Dead" (*BR*, 46; *SP*, 27), a depiction of a rather macabre celebration held annually in Tehauntepec. Hayden, as the outsider observing a sort of grim gaiety, notes the way in which the floral sensuousness of the celebrants competes in a desperate contrast with death's harsh reality. Vultures "hover / in skies intense as voyeur's gazing," just as the past hovers over the present, a brief time given over "to the returning dead," as if those dead did not reside always in the consciousness of a people remembering so hard to forget.

Sensitive to the implications of history, Hayden does not require traditional activity to trigger his imagination. He responds even to inanimate artifacts and empty architecture. "Idol" (*BR*, 50; *SP*, 31), for example, results from the poet's viewing of a statue of an Aztec goddess. The poem sketches briefly in surrealistic description the human sacrifice once accorded this idol. Hayden in his own fashion dramatically imposes the past upon the present through the silent synesthesia of gruesome visual images expressed in the language of hearing: "soundless drumthrob of the heart wrenched / from the living breast, / of the raw meaty heart quivering in copal / smoke its praise." Hayden observes in another "artifact" poem that although these old gods are gone, and remain only as relics, the Aztec spirit is somehow more real than the surviving physical trappings of Christianity in some Mexican locales. He wrote "*Sub Specie Aeternitatis*" ("Under the Aspect of Eternity") (*BR*, 52; *SP*, 32) after touring a deserted convent in Tepoztlán. He locates the convent under the aspect of the "plangent fire" of the sun, a central symbol in Aztec religion, a symbol Hayden uses variously in many of his Mexican poems. Here the timeless sun emphasizes the self-defeat of Spanish conquest and the ultimate futility of imposed Christianity. Here in Tepoztlán the pagan gods are still present, as witnessed by the "silence of / a conquered and / defiant god" whose temple is now no more than a tourist attraction.

Perhaps influenced by the feelings conveyed in "*Sub Specie Aeternitatis*," Hayden dropped "El Cristo" (*BR*, 51), an impressionistic description of a locally created, grotesque statue of Jesus, when he compiled materials for *Selected Poems*. He added instead another brief portrait that is more dramatic than descriptive. "Kid" (*SP*, 35) proves a happy "substitution," since this short poem adds yet another striking figure to Hayden's collection of memorable characters. The "kid" is a streetwise little boy Hayden used to see in Cuernavaca, begging at the sidewalk cafés haunted by tourists and note-taking poets. "Found with homeless dogs / that worry sidewalk cafes," this little beggar shares with those dogs more than territory. He has clever "tricks of pathos for / the silly foreigners," yet is "deft and quick and accustomed" enough to dance beyond the reach of angry waiters. In spite of his spirit and resiliency, one senses that the "kid" cannot laugh and scamper the rest of his life, and although Hayden wisely forebears social moralizing, he does imbue this character sketch with an austere poignancy.

Hayden patterned his "Kid" after a particular street urchin, but he observed many more "ragged boys" on the streets and in the open markets of Mexico. He includes them in another poem as part of a larger picture, a picture he titles "Market" (*BR*, 53–54; *SP*, 33–34), a poem he summarized thusly:

I wanted, clearly, to describe the market, with its color, its activity, its exotic atmosphere, it squalor. Yet I was after more than the merely picturesque. The market scene focuses impressions, certain feelings I had about

Mexico—the harshness of existence for the poor, the indifference, or seeming indifference, to human misery I so often encountered there, the cruelty and beauty inherited from the past.

Among a veritable plethora of local color, Hayden stresses paradoxical images and injects human interaction of ironic contrast, both in illustration of those impressions he later listed in the above prose statement. With copious detail the poet juxtaposes the appetizing and disgusting aspects of the scene; for every plus there is a minus. The market offers confections and lush tropical fruit, but the sweet gelatins are "acid-green / and bloody" in color; the papayas are "too ripe"; the oranges are "rotting"; flowers leave "trampled / peony droppings." Within this setting Hayden enacts the central ironical drama—a confrontation between "the barefoot cripple" and the foreign tourists from whom he begs. Crawling "among rinds, orts / chewed butts, trampled / peony droppings," the beggar repeats his litany, "por caridad, por caridad" ("have charity"), as he crawls also among discomfited onlookers. The beggar's other voice, an interior monologue of contemptuous envy of the tourists' health and wealth, fairly leaps from the page, as it draws the reader's attention from the cluttered stage to a soliloquy of human misery. Hayden closes the scene by citing a final item in the market's inventory, a tin mask of an ancient Aztec god, figuratively overseeing the drama just described. For the poet this mask symbolizes the ironic confluence of misery and beauty, which he perceives as central in Mexico's ambience of a vital yet vitiated past. The figure of the Fire Mask was once a worshiped idol in pagan ritual; now the god exists as a cheap replica sold to mitigate poverty. Hayden said the mask "can be interpreted as representing the dead, yet living, past of the Mexican Indian and the powerlessness of the old gods to help him."

Perhaps the least typical and most telling of the Mexican poems is "Veracruz" (*BR*, 47–48; *SP*, 29–30). Hayden invoked Walt Whitman in describing hopes for a restorative stay in Mexico, suggesting he wanted to "loaf and invite the soul." But he could not escape himself; every place was home, yet he often felt alienated in his own company. In "Veracruz" he reports reaching and passing through an emotional crisis involving these hopes and fears. To pass through, he rends the veil, grasps for an ultimate reality beyond life.

In a descriptive first section Hayden locates himself at the harbor of this seaport city on a quiet afternoon, isolated in the midst of the idling Sunday crowd. His own walk takes him to the seaward end of the harbor, where the "shore / seen across the marbling waves" appears miragelike in "ornately green" concealment of "the inward-falling slum, / the stains and dirty tools of struggle." Hayden ponders these disparities among appearance and reality, concluding that "Here only the sea is real." Paradoxically, he views the sea, that timeless, traditional symbol of eternity, as a means of personal extinction. The sea presents him the opportunity to reject life's fantasy in exchange for a reality beyond deception. On the promontory he faces that choice:

> *Leap now*
> *and cease from error.*
> *Escape. Or shoreward turn,*
> *accepting all—*
> *the losses and farewells,*
> *the long warfare with self,*
> *with God.*

Hayden retains the present-tense immediacy in Section II to indicate the momentary passage of crisis. Once having made his choice, even the sea's reality becomes a mirage ("Thus reality / become unbearably a dream"). "Accepting all" is accepting life, including one's limited ability to pierce its veil. As the "multifoliate sea" becomes "phantasmal space," even this personal apocalypse dissipates, like a distant star, a "farewell image" that "burns and fades and burns."

Although the psychic stimulus behind "Veracruz" seems diametrically opposed to that of John Keats's "When I have fears that I may cease to be," Hayden's poem resembles the Keats sonnet both in locale and "method" for contemplating death. Hayden too stands alone "on the shore / Of the wide world" and "thinks" until life's uncertainties diminish in significance, fading "light years away" from a higher reality. For all its intimacy, Hayden's poem is essentially anonymous in its narrative technique. His "psychic distancing" takes the form of invisible narration; even the italicized interior voice debating death and life is disassociated, unattributed. Yet "Veracruz," unlike other Mexican poems, looks inward—Hayden bares, rather than "invites" his soul. Otherwise, the "Inference of Mexico" segment presents a people viewed through the poetic prism of cultural history and individualized humanity. This outward perspective more nearly represents Hayden's sensibility in general application, as further evidenced by his cumulative collection of poetry addressing his own cultural history.

## Heritage

Hayden's sustained concern with black history and culture can be adduced from the unbroken span of work in this vein reproduced in *A Ballad of Remembrance* and *Selected Poems*. A brief sampler of such poems reaches from "O Daedalus, Fly Away Home," first "printed" as an entry in the 1942 Hopwood "Black Spear" manuscript, to "Runagate Runagate," finally revised as late as 1964. A wide diversity of technical modes rivals in range this chronological span. Hayden explored his heritage with tenacious methodical research and expressed his findings and feelings in poetic forms that include fusions of classical myth, local lore and folk music ("Daedalus"), dramatic monologue ("The Ballad of Nat Turner"), montages of narrative voices ("Runagate"), quasi-epic themes and structures ("Middle Passage"), and innovative adaptation of the traditional sonnet ("Frederick Douglass").

"O Daedalus, Fly Away Home" (*BR*, 67; *SP*, 71) illustrates Hayden's early propensity toward, and skill in weaving together, disparate materials in a kaleidoscopic display of craft, knowledge, and feeling. Struck by the almost archetypal similarity between the Icarus-Daedalus myth and the Georgia Sea Island legend of the Flying African, the poet combines those myths in the contrapuntal rhythms of juba dances one associates with the slavery era of the antebellum South. He uses varied voices to evoke slave aspirations for escape and freedom via literal flight back to Africa. Through incantatory repetition and shifts in his trochaic accentuation, Hayden merges also the dancers and the dance. Expressive of recurrent ritual, the repetition of the "fly away home" refrain, drawn from a Negro spiritual, reminds the reader of the slaves' steadfast longing for freedom. Contrarily, the rhythmic shifts vary the emotional tone between long-term anxiety and the momentary escape of dancing in abandoned gaiety.

## Heritage—"Middle Passage"

Hayden's early *magnum opus* has its origins in the same career era and creative tendencies as "Daedalus." "Middle Passage" (*BR*, 60–66; *SP*, 65–70), probably Hayden's most famous heritage poem, grew out of his research work and the "Black Spear" project of the late 1930s and early 1940s.[3] Notable for its broad sweep of black history, and striking for its virtuoso blending of narrative voices, the poem is especially intriguing in its generic features.[4] Hayden's epic aspirations warrant special scrutiny in view of the poem's content, structure, tone, and theme. "Middle Passage" bears virtually all the tracings of an epic in miniature, but it is neither conventional nor mocking in its epic mode. While Hayden employs most of the "standard" epic conventions and devices, he consistently and ironically inverts or alters these features. Through this inversion technique, he creates what could be called an "anti-epic," an original form with which he achieves a coherent merger of formal technique and poetic theme. His "antiepic" approach includes characterization. With it he brings to life and ennobles Cinquez, an "antihero" and a symbolic racial representative whom Hayden glorifies in celebrating the ultimate subject of the poem— the heroic struggle for freedom by the black victims of the "Middle Passage."[5]

Some of Hayden's ironic inversions of epic elements are rather direct and apparent; others are more subtle and have profound thematic implications. In the former category, the poet does not begin the poem with a direct statement of epic theme but instead with a brief but appalling catalog of slave ships: "*Jesus, Estrella, Esperanza, Mercy.*" These pleasant names and those that follow in line fourteen ("*Desire, Adventure, Tartar, Ann*") initiate the tone of cosmic irony that permeates the entire poem. Hayden's research shows in his deliberate use of historically factual Spanish and English names. Thus through historical selectivity Hayden emphasizes a situational irony that is as real as it is literary. The poet-narrator, in subsequently describing these symbolic ships, points up this irony: "Their bright ironical names / like jests of kindness on a murderer's mouth" (ll. 96–97).

Those ships also figure centrally in the formal statement of theme, tersely injected early in the narrative:

> Middle Passage:
> voyage through death
> to life upon these shores. (5–7)

The classic epic premise of a quest-journey is thus established, but in terms that are uniquely Hayden's. He uses "death" in a literal sense to counterpoint ironically the figurative use of "life." As his narrative account makes clear, "death" as a part of the journey is no more horrible a prospect than the life to be "lived" after arrival. The transit through the Middle Passage is indeed a "voyage through death," but the life of slavery to be experienced by the survivors will be a living death, a death in life.

Hayden thus frequently includes, but inverts, denies, or uses ironic substitutes for, the typical epic conventions and devices. His treatment of the supernatural element further exemplifies this technique. The "gods" are present in the poem, but neither as fickle pagan deities with vested interests in human endeavor nor as providential protectors in a "Christian" epic. Instead, Hayden confronts the reader with two alternate pseudosupernatural influences: indifferent brute nature, or pious hypocritical Puritanism. The sharks who hungrily await the suicidal leaps of crazed slaves are also identified as the "tutelary gods" of the harassed or endangered slavers (12–13; 31–33). These gods "intervene" in that they provide a quick death to the suffering victims of the Middle Passage and ironically serve as guardians and instructors to those responsible for that suffering. These "grinning" gods accompany the slave ships in mockery of both slaves and slavers, and with their pointed presence in the poem Hayden mocks the supernatural role in "ordinary" epics.

The Christian element in the poem also seethes with irony. The poet is quite clear about his intent here:

Irony is a constant element through the poem. The reference to Christianity in this section [Section I], the lines from the hymn, emphasize the irony of the Christian acceptance and justification of the slave trade as a means of bringing "heathen souls" to Christ.[6]

Hayden refers to a hymn entitled "Jesus, Savior, Pilot Me," parts of which he weaves between the narrative segments of Part I as an ironic refrain.[7] For example, lines from that hymn bracket the brief

stanza that represents a prayer for God's blessing upon slave ships
departing from New England for the west coast of Africa:

> Jesus   Savior   Pilot   Me
> Over   Life's   Tempestuous   Sea
>
> We pray that Thou wilt grant, O Lord,
> safe passage to our vessels bringing
> heathen souls unto Thy chastening.
>
> Jesus   Savior

By enclosing this three-line stanza with lines and phrases from the
hymn Hayden evokes an atmosphere where slave trading was ra-
tionalized as a missionary rather than as a commercial venture. The
poet also sets off subsequent narrative passages with more phrases
from the same hymn ("Thou Who Walked on Galilee" [46],
"Pilot Oh Pilot Me" [69]), thereby juxtaposing religious sentiments with details of horrible events and immoral carnage aboard
slave ships, in order to emphasize the perverted application of
Christian doctrine to human inhumanity. God exists neither as a
source of hope for the enslaved nor as a divine "pilot" for seagoing
Christians, but merely as an excuse to justify cruel exploitation of
one group of human beings by another.

     In denying the presence of Christian love through his treatment
of the supernatural, Hayden characteristically provides a thematic
alternative with a metaphoric basis. The slave ships negotiate the
Middle Passage with navigational aids quite in contrast to God's
blessing. The "voyage through death" is a "voyage whose chart-
ings are unlove" (102–3), where "horror is the corposant and com-
pass rose" (4).[8] The narrator calls the slave ships "Shuttles in the
rocking loom of history" (94), and as these "dark ships move" to
weave the fabric of history, their courses are governed not by divine
providence but by inhumanity and horror.

     Thus, in effect, God does not exist in "Middle Passage." When
the poem is compared with traditional epics, this omission is
notable because the presence of God or gods in such poems has
often verified the favored status of the central character or epic hero.
Indeed, only relatively late in Hayden's poem is the reader even introduced to the central character, and then the poet presents the

hero both belatedly and indirectly. Hayden's treatment of the conventional epic concern for the fate and accomplishments of a prominent national or racial hero is probably the most thematically significant of his "epic inversions."

Cinquez, as an epic hero, demands special attention because with this character Hayden posits the primary message of the poem. Although the manner of Cinquez's presentation and his social stature as an epic hero are unorthodox, this character emerges as the spiritual symbol of the suffering and aspirations of his race. Cinquez becomes a "deathless primaveral image"; his is a "life that transfigures many lives" (177); his characterization is one of epic dimension achieved through an antiepic mode. Since the narrative premise of the epic as a distinct genre involves the telling of a story that accounts the exploits of a prominent and noble warrior, such stories usually introduce the hero early in the telling. The "epic hero" of "Middle Passage" is not introduced until line 138 of a poem 179 lines in length. In the remaining forty-two lines Hayden provides an ironically indirect account of Cinquez's "adventures," establishes the character as central to the narrative structure and theme of the entire poem, and climaxes the heroic portrayal by identifying Cinquez as the ultimate symbol of the timeless human desire for freedom, a theme of epic proportion.[9]

Hayden attributes personal nobility to Cinquez by combining history with art, by confusing myth, legend, and fact. Although Cinquez clearly was the leader of the *Amistad* mutiny and was put on trial in that role (in the case of the *United States, Appelants*, v. *Cinque, and Others, Africans*), he was a rice planter, not a chieftain or a prince. As a leader of slaves in rebellion against their captors, he gave his followers hope and direction, but contemporary events, curiosity, and sympathy elevated him to "regal" status. Public curiosity was abetted by an idealized portrait done by Nathaniel Jocelyn,[10] a phrenological profile,[11] and by several sympathetic newspaper editorials in praise of Cinquez, e.g., "The more we learn of the man's character . . . the more are we impressed with a sense of his possessing the true elements of heroism."[12] The abolitionists who took up the cause of the "Amistaders" regarded Cinquez as a "noble savage" and saw his situation as an opportunity to set a legal precedent that would forward the abolition movement.

Hayden retains these historical perspectives and then transcends them by portraying Cinquez in symbolic terms of epic scope. Cinquez's desire and struggle for freedom become the "deep immortal human wish, / the timeless will" (174–75). Ultimately, then, "Middle Passage" creates a hero who represents his race in a quest for personal liberty, something in which all men have a real shared interest. Hayden's hero remains central to the entire narrative because Cinquez is the symbolic personification of the primary theme of the poem. Hayden makes the hero appear larger than life because his "life transfigures many lives." Cinquez's rebellion against enslavement thus stands for the physical and spiritual struggle for freedom by all blacks then and since.

"Middle Passage" is epic in theme and import although "anti-epic" in formal structure and technique. Due to Hayden's manner of ironically contrasting his style with traditional epic characteristics, the poem fairly reverberates with unanticipated thematic implications throughout its length. If "unlove" provides the direction for imposed travel through the Middle Passage, then irony is the thematic gloss for reader progress toward an understanding and appreciation of Hayden's epic tribute. This indirect and muted treatment of a horrible chapter in human history at once demonstrates the poet's developing craftsmanship, verifies his compassionate objectivity (his "negative capability," one might say), and substantiates Robert Hayden's own humanity.

## Heritage—Nat Turner, Harriet Tubman, Frederick Douglass

His portrayal of another racial hero is more of a psychological profile than an historical narrative. Hayden would later use the term "psychogram" to designate poems like "The Ballad of Nat Turner" (BR, 68–70; SP, 72–74). He portrays Nat Turner's visionary character in dramatic-monologue format, reconstructing imaginatively Turner's "own" words in description of his vision of warring angels, a "shared" vision that has the effect of characterizing the speaker. Hayden thus presents a revelation within a revelation. He effectively incorporates the speaker's unconscious revelation of his own psyche as Turner addresses his followers in a purposeful summary of his personal revelation of divine direction.

In his use of highly stylized language Hayden stresses Turner's

otherworldly concerns and suggests the source of his charismatic effect upon his "brethren." Astutes choices in stanza pattern and
prosody augment these aspects of characterization. The quatrains
with their slant rhymes suggest Turner's personality as well as his
powers of persuasion. As he recounts his revelation in detail, the
speaker's language reveals that his fanatical faith derives from a
sense of fearful awe. The poet thereby subtly implies that Turner
could inspire similar responses in his listener-followers.

Hayden highlights the singularity of Turner's person and the
power of his vision through the emphasis of contrast; he shows the
speaker in frightened solitude before the revelation and portrays
him with a sense of messianic purpose afterwards. Nat first describes
himself wandering alone in the "scary night," "afraid and
lonely." He reports encountering the suspended corpses of Ibo war-
riors, spirits which soon vanish to be replaced by "seething shapes /
of evil" that leave him reeling in fear. Even the central revelation,
his witnessing of the celestial combat, he describes as "fearful
splendor" from which he seeks to hide. But when he "beheld the
conqueror faces" and saw "they were like mine," the terror is
mitigated with joy. Praising Jehovah, his "honer, and harshener,"
Turner overcomes his fear, and falls into a trancelike sleep. When
he awakes, "at last free / And purified," Turner returns to his slave
status with a sense of divine mission, content to bide his time in
awaiting God's signal for the insurrection he would later lead.

Hayden thus provides psychological insight into history, implicitly accounting for Nat Turner's motivation on the basis of religious
fantaticism. The poet objectively withholds explicit moral judgment or endorsement, but leaves no doubt of Turner's genuine
belief in ordained mission. Although the portrait is imaginatively
created rather than factually documented, Hayden's extensive
research prompted this particular conception of Turner as an individualized personality. Whether Turner's obsession with freedom
led him to fanatical religiosity, or vice versa, Hayden's "Ballad"
captures the quintessence of that connection within the imagined
psychology of this intriguing historical figure.

The poem predates William Styron's *The Confessions of Nat
Turner* (1966), but unlike that controversial novel, "The Ballad of
Nat Turner" has received little or no attention from either black or
white critics. Such neglect is doubly unfortunate because Hayden's
version of Nat Turner could almost arbitrate the disagreement be-

tween black and white scholars on the legitimacy of Styron's fictional portrayal of Turner. In 1968, for example, in the wake of "establishment" critical acclaim for the novel, a body of black scholars and critics reached the perhaps expectable and certainly justified conclusion that Styron presents Turner as a psychological cripple, one stereotyped by a bizarre obsession with interracial sex.[13] However, the same group of black writers would portray Turner almost as falsely, converting the racial hero into a militant revolutionary with no hint of psychological eccentricity. One version falsifies Turner's character entirely; the other would demystify him, reducing his motivation to the "ordinary" ("Every slave is a potential revolutionary"). Admittedly, Hayden's Turner is as "created" as Styron's, but the poet accounts for the historical facts of Turner's religiosity and his rebellious motivation in terms that are more psychologically plausible. Ironically, of the ten black writers who jointly contend that "Nat Turner still awaits a literary interpreter worthy of his sacrifice," only one of them even acknowledges the existence of Robert Hayden's portrait of this pioneer in the struggle for black freedom.

Hayden's tribute to Harriet Tubman depicts another sort of struggle for freedom. "Runagate Runagate" (*SP*, 75–77), like "Middle Passage," derives from the formative stages of the 1942 "Black Spear" project, but the poet's close knowledge of its subject matter originated in his 1936–38 WPA research on the Underground Railroad. During that era he had literally dramatized his admiration of Harriet Tubman in his play about her, "Go Down, Moses," and he later quite naturally included her in his planned "Black Spear" collection of racial heroes. An early version of "Runagate" appeared in the Hughes-Bontemps anthology in 1949. Only slightly better satisfied with the poem than he had been with the play, Hayden thereafter set "Runagate" aside until Rosey Pool's 1963 reading in Nashville. Inspired by her fondness for the poem, and in response to her request to reprint it in her collection *I Am the New Negro*, Hayden sent Dr. Pool a "completely new version" in 1964.[14] That substantially improved version proved definitive; it was to be reprinted in *Selected Poems* two years later and appears most recently in the comprehensive *Angle of Ascent* (1975).

"Runagate Runagate" shares structural similarity as well as era of origin with "Middle Passage," in that Hayden incorporates a mon-

tage of narrative voices and materials to describe group struggle for
freedom and to highlight a racial heroine. Partitioning the poem
into two narrative sections, Hayden leads from the general subject of
covert northern migration before and during the Civil War to the
specific praise of Harriet Tubman as the heroic conductor of the
Underground Railroad. He skillfully equates the slaves' yearning
for freedom and their physical flight toward it by setting in motion
at the outset of the poem a particular but clearly representative
"runagate" (a runaway, fugitive slave). As the anonymous escaped
slave runs on, so do those lines depicting his headlong pursuit of
that ultimate destination. In seven rather lengthy lines of run-on
narration, without medial, much less end-stop, punctuation,
Hayden reverberates sound and sense:

> Runs falls rises stumbles on from darkness into darkness
> and the darkness thicketed with shapes of terror
> and the hunters pursuing and the hounds pursuing
> and the night cold and the night long and the river
> to cross and the jack-muh-lanterns beckoning beckoning
> and blackness ahead and when shall I reach that somewhere
> morning and keep on going and never turn back and keep on going

With repetition in phrasing and connectives, using "and" twelve
times in those seven lines, Hayden sharpens the image of a fugitive
slave pounding ahead while trembling with fear.

The pulsating rhythm of this initial segment continues throughout the poem, at times accomplished with inserted repetition
(chanting) of the key term "runagate," but more frequently by
weaving excerpts from slave spirituals and protest songs through the
narrative fabric. One can identify at least half a dozen such songs,
all deliberately selected and edited to extend the thematic unity of
"crossing over," "bound for freedom," determined "to be free."
The other montage materials in that first section add the effect of
"other" voices. For example, a facsimile of an owner's advertisement for return of escaped slaves summarizes the "establishment"
perspective of slaves as no more than chattel, and of owners as no
less than beleaguered keepers. Of course, the elusiveness of escaped
slaves, so troublesome for pursuing owners, only heightens the
sense of determined urgency in the slaves' viewpoint. Hayden
stresses this aspect by framing the advertisement with protest folk-

song excerpts that avow escape from the life implicitly described in the owner's handbill. The poet leads up to the facsimile text with the excerpt "No more auction block for me / no more driver's lash for me" and follows it with "and before I'll be a slave / I'll be buried in my grave." This basic narrative pattern of sustained pointing with black antislavery sentiment, alternated with brief counterpointing of proslavery materials, prevails throughout the poem.

Introduced through omniscient narration in the second section, Harriet Tubman is immediately characterized in mythic, symbolic terms as a "woman of earth, whipscarred / a summoning, a shining." Hayden next personalizes and lends immediacy to her portrait with an episodic anecdote related by another anonymous "runagate" who describes a typical ride on Tubman's railroad. This speaker freely acknowledges that when her followers despaired, she literally forced them at gunpoint to continue their escape ("you keep on going now, or die she says"). Hayden gives Tubman her due historic recognition through the indirect emphasis of his montage technique, reproducing the ostensible text of a "wanted" poster that lists her aliases as "The General" and "Moses" and labels her a "Stealer of Slaves" in league with the prominent abolitionists of the times also listed. Her threat to the enemies of freedom, and thus her glory among her followers and admirers, is subtly manifest in the clipped phrasing of her fugitive status: "Armed and known to be Dangerous / Wanted   Reward   Dead or Alive."

In spite of such "static" materials, Hayden somehow sustains the feeling of continuous movement over the entire length of "Runagate." He once more picks up the rhythmic pace to close the poem. With an italicized segment of mythic narrative, in the mode of similar passages in "Middle Passage," he merges the railroad of Harriet Tubman's making with the "glory train" so often sung about in the spirituals:

> *Oh that train, ghost-story train*
> *through swamp and savanna movering movering,*
> *over trestles of dew, through caves of the wish,*
> *Midnight Special on a sabre track movering movering,*
> *first stop Mercy and the last Hallelujah.*

Hayden's original spiritual lyric fuses the physical flight northward to freedom and the human aspiration that prompts it. Like his other heritage poem of mixed narrative voices, "Runagate Runagate" celebrates the black struggle to be free and pays tribute to another inspirational leader active in that cause. Appropriately, Tubman's presence echoes at the conclusion in the repeated refrain "Come ride-a my train. . . . Come ride-a my train."

Although "Frederick Douglass" (*BR*, 71; *SP*, 78) does not appear in *The Lion and the Archer*, Hayden chose its subject as part of the "Black Spear" project and first published this accentual sonnet in 1947 during his experimental "Baroque Period."[15] The poem, since widely anthologized for its admirable features as a heritage portrait of a racial hero, stands as one of the poet's best examples of successful innovation. Hayden divests himself of practically all the traditional formal conventions associated with the sonnet, yet retains the reinforcement relationship between form and meaning, a relationship traditionally facilitated by elements of conventional form such as rhyme, specified meter, and prescribed structural divisions.[16]

With a first reading, "Frederick Douglass" may seem a sonnet in name only. The lines do not rhyme; the meter is clearly not iambic pentameter; although the poem has the "required" fourteen lines, it appears nonstructured or at least free of structural restraint. But the appearance is deceptive; the sonnet is in fact highly structured. The primary basis of this structure is in sentence type and syntactical arrangement. The sonnet consists of only two sentences. The first of these covers line one through the midpoint of line eleven; the second sentence spans the remainder of the poem. Both are periodic sentences, with the vital elements withheld until the last moment. This choice of sentence type allows Hayden to build toward the ultimate point of the sentences (and the poem) while controlling the tone of the preceding clauses. In the first periodic sentence the poet twice utilizes parallelism, whereby he first presents and expands his conception of freedom and then follows with a personal and historical profile of Douglass. The second sentence concludes the sonnet by distinguishing between tributes to the memory of Douglass and the ultimate nature of his legacy.

The parallel structure of the first sentence is used to define freedom repeatedly and progressively. Hayden with a series of descriptive terms forms a progression that moves "freedom" from the realm of the abstract to the concrete and real. This movement mirrors and thus reinforces the movement and meaning of the entire sonnet. The series contains words made equivalent (but not identical) with freedom: in line one, "this freedom" is followed by "this liberty," which expands the conception of freedom only slightly, from one abstraction to another (albeit more specific) abstraction. "This beautiful and terrible thing" advances the definition one more step toward the concrete.

That this seemingly indescribable "thing" is being methodically defined becomes apparent with the next step in the progression, a shift to freedom's elemental function. This shift (a use of Aristotle's "final cause") images freedom as palpable as dirt; freedom is as "needful to man as air," and although air is invisible, the concreteness of "usable as earth" brings "freedom" full scale to an elemental reality. Just as Hayden with parallel structure and descriptive diction moves freedom from abstraction to reality, so his poem contends that Douglass's legacy ultimately will be the reality of freedom lived rather than freedom only conceived. The delayed climax of this lengthy periodic sentence thus exhibits, in miniature, the thrust of the entire poem. The form is the function is the meaning.

The final sentence (lines 11–14) climaxes the sonnet and completes the portrait by clarifying *how* Douglass will be remembered *when* freedom is real rather than abstract. Hayden again uses a parallel structure; this time to facilitate antithesis. He creates a set of balanced contrasts that distinguish the real, but artificial, heritage from the living, breathing fulfillment of Douglass's dream. The real heritage left by Douglass is not fame commemorated or maintained with artifacts, but rather the living progeny of his example. The items in the "not" phrases are contrasted with the items in the "but" phrases as Hayden's rhetorical strategy for clarifying the difference between superficial reality (statues, legends, poems, wreathes) and living reality ("lives grown out of his life, the lives / fleshing his dream"). This assertion of how Douglass shall be remembered thus culminates the movement of the poem as it completes the overall progression from the abstract conception to the accomplished reality. This conclusion derives organically from the general "when . . . then" premise of the sonnet. By implicitly including his own poem among those other forms of artifice, Hayden subtly but decisively acknowledges that such freedom has not yet "arrived." Indeed, he wrote the poem out of longing for a time and a reality of freedom when his masterful sonnet, and other tributes to Douglass like it, would be simply superfluous.

For all their diversity of technique and mode, Hayden's mid-career heritage poems stretch a skein of consistency in their tone and treatment of theme. Supported by meticulous historical research, the poet resurrects notable heroic figures in creative portrayals and posits these individualized characters as the symbolic, representative means to celebrate the suffering and achievement of the race in general. This mode verifies through illustration the poet's view of history as an inseparable fusion of past and present while it allows him to note those personalities who have altered the currents of history's ever-flowing river. More and more as he matured as a poet, Hayden would return to his more immediate heritage as subject matter for his work; increasingly, he would concentrate on characterization dramatized through single or multiple voices. Ultimately those voices are his voice; their histories are his history, as poems of cultural heritage and personal memory almost imperceptively merge in a culminating intersection of the long parallel paths of the past.

## Transcendence

In many ways a romantic in the most profound sense, Robert Hayden was fascinated with the realities lurking beneath the surfaces of certainty and mystery. Although he was both emotionally and intellectually convinced that a spiritual imminence linked this "fact and fantasy," nevertheless he continually scrutinized his own experience for answers that could never be final. Hayden often acknowledged the difficulty of maintaining this personal "negative capability," that state of being content in the face of uncertainty. Indeed, he was still calling himself a "skeptical believer" in the final few months of his life.

Some poems from his early collections indirectly announce this perspective by describing life as viewed through it. A few are artistic efforts to capture the constantly changing surfaces of life. Others rather directly express Baha'i religious views, acknowledging a higher, spiritual reality and presenting a view of life that derives from his faith in the certainty of a divine providential hand in all change, whether large or small, tragedy or triumph. Sometimes Hayden peers hard at mundane reality, sensing an unseen significance; sometimes he struggles with himself to view human cruelty and suffering as part of a larger, ultimately benevolent scheme. Such poems from *A Ballad of Remembrance* and *Selected Poems* are few in number but highly representative in content and perspective.

The poet uses the phrase "the striptease of reality" in "Theme and Variation" (*BR*, 40; *SP*, 59) to sum up the concurrent appeal and frustration of communion with material nature. The poem is about transformation, both in content and theme. Hayden tries to capture reality by contemplating "changing permanence," an eternally recurring phenomenon where "all things alter" even as one "stops" them with cognizance. Hayden explores the paradoxical thematic notion that everything that is, is on the verge of becoming something else, through the use of a remarkably apt set of oxymorons. With them he daringly provides a description of constancy derived only from constant variation. After inclusively cataloging "all things" as "Fossil, fuschia, mantis, man / fire and water, earth and air," he proceeds to characterize this world of altering states with a series of oxymorons connoting dynamic stasis: "revelling shadows," "changing permanence," "lurking rush," and "sly transcience." Even that "striptease of reality" is glimpsed only from the corner of an eye. In sum, all things, when known, become unknown. The speaker attributes this phenomenal reality to God, but includes both the comfort and distress inherent in this attribution. God may alter light to darkness, but it is a "rainbow darkness," a darkness wherein man is both enlightened and dismayed by a divine force that "waylays us and empowers" [us].

Hayden includes also his personal disjunction between conviction and skepticism within the unique narrative format. A first-person speaker declares his immediate responses of sense and belief, but those are in turn reported (but not directly quoted) and displaced by a third-person narrator who calls the first speaker "the stranger." This duality of perspective, developed in the first section of the short poem, gives way in the final segment to a "pure" first-person narrative. Whether this final speaker's faith is Hayden's or whether the poet leaves this "stranger" to his own subjectivity is never made clear. That ambiguity may well be deliberate—at least it would be quite appropriate in the conclusion of a poem about the vagaries of reality by a poet who called himself a "skeptical believer."

A similar duality informs Hayden's earliest poetic attempt to cope with his horror at human suffering by hoping against hope in his belief in the Baha'i Faith. Significantly, he shifted titles between printings of the resultant poem. The original title, "In light half nightmare and half vision" (*BR*, 42), indicates that ambivalence of feeling, and the final title, "From the Corpse Woodpiles, From the Ashes" (*SP*, 60), describes the stark products of human depravity. Hayden pictures himself in the poem encircled by the unredeemed deaths of countless fellow humans. Approaching him during a nightmarish dream, they come from "the staring pits of Dachau / Buchenwald they come . . . From Johannesburg, from Seoul." Horrified by the prospect of what man has done to man, and aghast that God has allowed it, Hayden seeks solace by contemplating the individual agony of his personal savior in the context of his Baha'i Faith. Like Jesus in the Christian faith, Baha'u'llah was "man beatified," the divine messenger of man's ultimate deliverance onto harmonious life and human brotherhood. Recalling Baha'u'llah's redemptive suffering reminds Hayden that the promised millennium of human harmony would be preceded by dark eras of chaotic evil and mass suffering. His faith thus affords him a transcendence, a "vision" with which to counter the all too recurrent nightmares.

Such restorative experience would be for the "skeptical believer" a desperate requirement during much of the turbulent 1960s. Although not so directly acknowledged in later poems, Hayden's precariously tenacious faith in a higher reality and an ultimate good would sustain his work in his next volume of poetry, aptly titled *Words in the Mourning Time* (1970).

## Chapter Five
# Breaking the Dark
## Body Politic and Poetic Spirit

The era of Robert Hayden's increasing prominence in the years following the success of *Selected Poems* (1966) was in many ways as trying for him as those times were for the country. Although gratified by that measure of appreciation for his work, he was deeply troubled by the unrest and violence erupting across the land. This compassionate yet helpless concern exacerbated his feelings of personal trial and alienation. Some of these feelings reflect themselves in his personal poems, especially those written and published at the height of what Hayden called "the mourning time," in general reference to the sociopolitical atmosphere in the country but also in specific reference to his own response to that atmosphere.

The work of this era, published as *Words in the Mourning Time* (1970) and *The Night-Blooming Cereus* (1972), shows the poet writing his way through a dark period in his life. In the first of these two collections, he atypically addresses directly the issues of war and civil violence, speaking out with the social fervor of his youth, but in the medium of his restrained, mature art. *Words* in other subject areas sometimes borders on despair, but even in his anguish Hayden more often seeks, and occasionally achieves, transcendence. *The Night-Blooming Cereus*, while less substantial in sheer volume, projects equally long shadows of darkness and light. If these two books can be grouped for discussion, it is because they both exhibit the poet's concerns for human suffering, endurance, and enlightenment. In this concern Hayden struggles constantly to find transcendent meaning. Some poems display a technical, artistic permanence of value; others approach or achieve a spiritual transcendence. Hayden himself would scarcely make such a distinction, since in his poetic credo the former could be a manifestation of the latter. In either case, Hayden's mature work of the early 1970s is difficult to organize according to oversimple categories of subject matter or technical variety. Although frequently expressive of agonizing perturbation, the poems convey a unity of moral vision so pervasive that often one is scarcely aware of distinctions among subject, form and meaning.

## Personals

In his earlier work Hayden had discreetly documented his personal emotional turmoil in such diversely symbolic poems as "The Web," "The Wheel," and "The Diver." In these instances he cites through figuration the existence of psychic anguish, hints at its nature (if not cause), and implies its recurrence. In a sense, he "updates" the category and yet concludes this sort of confessional lyric with "Sphinx" in *Words in the Mourning Time* (11). Therein the poet beholds himself held captive by the Sphinx, fated to endure her riddling as a "psychic joke" he will never understand. Viewing himself as a victim of cruel caprice, Hayden nonetheless accepts his status, indicating he has learned to live with the reality he accepted in "Vera Cruz." The poet suggests this acceptance by giving the silent Sphinx a voice, in which she assures him he will in time grow accustomed to his quandary, even to view it with "a certain pained amusement." Of course, in writing the poem, that is precisely what Hayden is doing. Just as self-evidently, the conundrum of Hayden's personal sphinx is passed on to the reader; he leaves the poem itself as a riddle, with no hint as to the specific situation or particular condition with which he must, and apparently can, live. Even in "personal" interviews, Hayden kept the "psychic joke" of "Sphinx" pretty much to himself, so the choice of figuration is ultimate, and this symbolic "final say" about his personal emotional torment is an especially appropriate conclusive "say."[1]

About some of his more particular concerns, he is more specific, but no less skillful in oblique expression. For example, he addresses his lingering crisis of identity with a "real" persona in " 'Mystery Boy' Looks for Kin in Nashville" (*WMT*, 14). Emotionally provoked by a factual newspaper account of a little lost girl who seemed not to know who she was or where she came from, Hayden identified with her situation. He reconstituted the news story to accommodate his own background and feelings, in effect allegorizing his own anxieties about identity.[2] Thus the "Puzzle faces in the dying elms" in their uneven treatment of the mystery boy could represent the acceptance and rejection Hayden experienced in both his early personal life and later professional career. Sometimes the faces "promise him treats"; "sometimes they hiss and spit at him." The mystery boy's source of comfort, identified as a "black doll" who is "his hidden bride," seems suggestive of Hayden's relationship with his wife, Erma. She too came to him in a "disremembered time," but the narrator associates the doll with "mimosa's fancy-work leaves and blooms," in significant contrast to the "dying elms," those "angry trees" that conceal, yet harbor, the "puzzle faces" with their ambiguous voices. Just as the lost boy clings to his doll, Hayden turns to his wife for solace and comfort. The "dollbaby wife" helps him cope with those haunting parental voices from his past, calling him, yet eluding or denying him. She assures him, "I know where they are, don't cry. / We'll go and find them, we'll go / and ask them for your name again." In effect, Mrs. Hayden's love and devotion provided the poet with an alternate identity in the absence of that lost earlier identity he could never quite either forget or retrieve.

If the circumstances of his youth denied Hayden the kind of familial love he then so craved, his devotion to his wife and daughter compensated. A very personal poem in commemoration of the birth of his daughter, Maia, illustrates both the extent of his love and the artistic merit intrinsic in its formal poetic expression. A "birthday poem" in a strikingly different sense of that often-maligned subgenre of occasional poetry, "October" (*WMT*, 57–59) subsumes its specific purpose because the poet implicitly establishes aesthetic priorities before he equates the timelessness of natural beauty and the temporal joy of human love. In the first of four brief stanzas Hayden gives the month of October its rightful place in the natural scheme of things by noting "its plangency, its glow," and by comparing the autumnal season to "words in / the poet's mind," and to "God in / the saint's" [mind]. Having indirectly established the beauty and importance of October in the reader's mind, the poet straightforwardly recounts in the second section his joy at Maia's birth on "that October morning," and their naming of her after a constellation and John Keats's "Ode to Maia." The devout father then simply declares his love for his daughter on her October birthday. Yet he concludes the segment by declaring that he writes the poem also to "say October / like the phoenix sings you." This equating of Maia and October accomplishes much more than a deft transition to the final two sections with their emphasis on seasonal signs. Therein Hayden characterizes October for its rebirth symbolism, manifest when the natural world transposes itself in a process he calls "deathless dying." Like the flaming phoenix, the burning "chimera colors" of fall, and even an early "surprising" snowfall, when reflecting the sun to "set / the snow on fire," presage renewed life and eternal existence. As Hayden's personal phoenix sings his daughter, the poet makes her birth and her life equivalent with that larger cycle, thereby subtly and gratefully recognizing the eternality of human love. In perceiving and expressing this most transcendent of themes in a most personal poem, Robert Hayden "proved" his point—with "October" he in effect immortalized Maia by enjoining her forever with the endless Octobers of life.

"October" represents a high point in the personal expression found in *Words in the Mourning Time*. "The Broken Dark" (*WMT*, 15) represents a low. Yet both poems conclude in a transcendent statement of faith. The title, "The Broken Dark," connotes both the darkness of Hayden's spiritual introspection and its eventual refraction into the shadowy light of uncertain faith. Indeed, this sort of imagery dominates the narrative. Lying sleepless and helpless in a "dark hospital room," the speaker stares "at shadows of a flower and its leaves" on the wall of a dimly lit corridor. He projects his metaphysical anxieties onto these shadow shapes, sensing good and evil as crucial aspects of an ephemeral "reality" and then contemplating his own life in terms of purpose or chaos. The specific question of purpose in his life leads to an inquiry about purpose in life generally. Viewing his own life "in the shadow of God's laser light," the speaker wonders if that light itself may be just another shadow, perhaps no more than a "shadow of deformed homunculus." He thus ponders the chaotic possibility that his life—indeed, all life—is just a shade of another shadow of our own fabrication, that man has created God by "deforming" man. If so, life becomes little more than "a fool's errand given by fools." This dark contemplation leads the speaker toward the temptation to despair. As he struggles for faith, he recalls other tests of fatih from Hebraic formulae ("Demons on the left. Death on either side, / the Rabbi said, the way of life between"), and possibly alludes to the martyrdom of Baha'u'llah ("I have come back / to tell thee of struggles in the pit"). In the midst of this internal struggle, the speaker notes also the immediate external reality of another patient's painful groaning and the rustling movement of the nightnurse.

Finally, he breaks the dark with enigmatic resolution: "Perhaps is dying." Left to determine whether Hayden means that uncertainty itself is a form of spiritual death, or that his own uncertainty is diminishing (his "perhaps" is dying), the reader can exclude neither interpretation, since the speaker concludes "free of pain," and yet with his "own death still / a theorem to be proved." And although he cites the healing spirit of the Baha'i Faith as the "forgiving cure" for the doubt and despair he has just described, one senses that while Hayden's dark has been "broken," it has not been dispelled entirely or permanently. Thus the "skeptical believer" contends that the ultimate realities of life and death remain theorems awaiting definitive proof, but his expectation of proof in itself constitutes a statement of faith, a belief that those hazy shadows are silhouettes of divine purpose.

## People

Only a relative few of the portrait poems in Hayden's two early 1970s publications originate in the time frame contemporary with their printing. However, this circumstance paradoxically evidences his continuing interest in "people poems," because those portraits of earlier origin are the most recently revised versions of poems that in varied forms have consistently appeared in successive collections dating back to 1955. These psychological profiles manifest other consistent yet developing characteristics of Hayden's perspective. Virtually all of the individualized characters share personal traits admired by their creator; many are ordinary people, or even "losers" or pariahs in society's eyes, who successfully cope with troubled lives through their enduring resiliency of temperament and strength of spirit.

Hayden's "Aunt Jemima of the Ocean Waves" (*WMT*, 18–21) exemplifies these generalizations about his long-term interest in portraiture of admired traits. Originally little more than a fragment, a brief section of a poem entitled "From the Coney Island Suite" published in *Figure of Time* (1955), the final version in

*Words* derives as much from the idea-theme of that fragment as it does from a real model for its central personage. Hayden called the original brief segment "Congress of Freaks." In it, he lists the "cast" of a Coney Island carnival sideshow (the "Unique Original Jemima / and Kokimo the Dixie Dancing Fool. . . . The snake-skinned man. / the boy with elephant face") and protests the "perverted logic" that makes confederates of physical freaks and racial stereotypes. The speaker disdains further consideration of the scene and turns away, "weary of this stale American joke."

In its more modern rendering, similar elements of setting, character, and authorial tone are almost entirely recast to emphasize character study and an empathetic understanding of the character. Aunt Jemima remains, and then some. She still wears the mask of outrageous racial stereotyping, and, as the introductory narrator realizes, is "enacting someone's notion of themselves / (and me)." Hayden, as this "new" narrator, again ponders the logic that groups together carnival freaks, blackface parodies, and himself, but this time he identifies more tolerantly, recognizing their roles as survival strategies: "Poor devils have to live somehow." After introducing Aunt Jemima (and himself) in those terms, the poet-speaker initiates the real portrait of this "heroine" through a subsequent encounter and dialogue between them on the Coney Island beach. By then out of her costume and role as Aunt Jemima, the woman, "her blue-rinsed hair / without the red bandana now," asks the narrator for a light, and soon explains that she spoke to him because he reminded her of a "friend" she once had. The dialogue quickly gives way to her monologue of reminiscence, wherein she recounts her life, love, and career.

Although her rambling discourse shows that she is totally self-aware of the irony in her present status, her account of how she arrived at this juncture is devoid of a sense of special self-merit for having endured. Therein lies the strength and subtlety of Hayden's portrait of her as an intriguing individual, and as an admired type. The detail of her autobiographical monologue illustrates these features of her portrayal. Gazing beyond the breakers toward the open sea, she recalls crossing the ocean long ago to "play" the major European capitals, billed as "The Sepia High Stepper," when "Crowned heads applauded me." With the world at her dancing feet, she found love to complement her fame and riches. But that "sweetest gentleman" was killed in World War I, and her "high-stepping" life ended with his. Reduced to survival tactics, she adopted another role, "Mysteria From / The Mystic East," reading palms and minds, "and telling suckers how to get / stolen rings and sweethearts back." But a night visit from the ghost of her dead lover aborts this "career"; in her reckoning, he "without a single word" silently warned her: "Baby, quit playing with spiritual stuff. " So she ended up with the sideshow, a "fake mammy to God's mistakes," in her phrasing, in her recognition of life's ironies.

Hayden closes the poem with a combination of direct narrative commentary and impressionistic figuration—a combination that extends the psychological portrait of this particular "Aunt Jemima" and suggests her racial and human significance. The narrator's response to her bemusement at her present self-deprecatory role in life reveals his understanding of her need both to shield and to mock herself. Her endurance depends on that detached perspective, that protective posture. The poet-speaker finds something noble in her self-sufficiency. The conjunction of her real person, her adopted role, and the ocean-resort locale brings to his mind "an antique etching" of "The Sable Venus," which he remembers "naked on / a baroque Cellini shell," a portrait he imagines symbolically equivalent to his romanticized vision of Aunt Jemima: "voluptuous / imago floating in the wake / of slave-ships on fantastic seas."

Of course neither the narrator-listener nor the poem's reader can be certain that Aunt Jemima's life story is not just another false image like the "sexual glitter" and "oppressive fun" of the beach carnival. The narrator rightly discerns that her laughter "shields" and "mocks" both herself and those enraptured by her story. Hayden jerks himself and the reader back from the "Sable Venus" reverie with a concluding balance between empathy and mere tolerance. Jemima has the last word; she sighs as she rises from the beach sand to return to her disguised life, but she takes her leave with the wisecracking attitude symptomatic of her resilient ability to cope: "Don't you take no wooden nickels, hear? / Tin dimes neither. So long, pal." As Hayden surely and carefully planned it, Aunt Jemima lingers in the reader's mind, an heroic figure regardless of whether she is wooden nickel, tin dime, or a true "Sable Venus."

Not coincidentally, another feminine figure of youthful spirit and indomitable endurance inspired Hayden's praise of those traits in the abstract, but poetically personified in allusion to a famous fictional dramatic character. He wrote "Lear Is Gay" (*WMT*, 62) in memory of Betsy Graves Reyneau, recalling her personal attributes to celebrate strength of spirit in old age.³ He lends prominence to the principle by citing Shakespeare's raging octogenerian, King Lear, from the play bearing his name. With Lear and Betsy in mind, the poet expresses his love of gaiety and laughter in "decreptitude." He begins with reference to another Shakespearean work, paraphrasing, or at least alluding to, those physical failings noted figuratively in Shakespeare's Sonnet 73, "That time of year thou mayst in me behold."⁴ Shakespeare's speaker figuratively deplores his advancing age by comparing bodily decline to the late fall "When yellow leaves, or none, or few, do hang / Upon those boughs which shake against the cold." The "gaiety" Hayden loves literally "has white hair / or thinning or none," and "has limbs askew / often as not." Hayden's "dimming sight" of old age also has its precedent in Shakespeare's quatrain comparing twilight and darkness to failing vision (ll. 5–8). Hayden uses the key phrase "can manage" to summarize a spirit that endures in spite of "fevers, rags / decreptitude." His Betsy Reyneau / King Lear–inspired figure not only "can manage" but "can laugh / sometimes / at time." One senses with this gay spirit the absurdity of life and perceives time not as a "grave" threat but as comparable to the ludicrous prospect of "A scarecrow whose / hobo shoulders are / a-twitch with crows." The simile Hayden carefully chooses to dramatize this trait seems to derive from another noted predecessor. Here he seems influenced by W. B. Yeats's earlier celebration of life's potential in "Sailing to Byzantium." Yeats also used a scarecrow image:

> An aged man is but a paltry thing,
> A tattered coat upon a stick, unless
> Soul clap its hands and sing, and louder sing
> For every tatter in its mortal dress.⁵

In "Lear Is Gay" Hayden thus thematically suggests that advancing age can enhance life, if and when the involuntary divestiture of external trappings allows the elderly a perception of reality afforded "unaccommodated" men like King Lear. Those like Betsy Reyneau, who enter that stage of life preequipped with gaiety of temperament and endurance of spirit, naturally achieve the clearest

vision and inspire in their younger contemporaries an appreciation
for renewed possibility. While "Lear Is Gay" indirectly eulogizes
Betsy Reyneau, the poem does not depict a particular individual in
personally unique terms. Rather, "Lear" evokes a potential assem-
blage of human exempla, a company the poet himself eventually
joined in his own old age.

Another portrait perhaps more closely reflects the chronological
and social context in which Hayden created it. Unlike the notions of
human relationship he explored in "Jemima" and "Lear," the
poet portrays in "Soledad" (*WMT*, 17) the total isolation and
alienation of a "convicted" drug addict. Hayden's ironic figuration
pictures the addict imprisoned by his habit in the cell of abject
loneliness, hiding out from a reality he can no longer face. The
anonymous persona convinces himself that his "jail" is his refuge.
Because "his fears and his unfinished self / await him down in the
anywhere streets,"

> He hides on the dark side of the moon,
> takes refuge in a stained-glass cell,
> flies to a clockless country of crystal.

Thus "cradled by drugs" in his regressive need to retreat from
unbearable life, he "connects" with the outside world only
through the medium of the jazz and blues music that seems to
speak to him alone. In his drug-deluded state, "Miles Davis cooly
blows for him," and Billie Holiday in her "red clay foxfire voice"
sings her sorrow at his pain. He is "no longer of that world," and
"only the ghost of Lady Day knows where / he is."

Hayden's "distanced" third-person narration includes no suggestion of sympathy or compassion for the addict. The poet's
deliberately aloof treatment of the subject is an effective rhetorical
strategy because it paradoxically deepens the reader's sense of waste
in the addict's "escape" into captivity. The ironic detachment of
this narrative mode thus heightens the sense of alienation implicit
in the poem's title and crucial to its theme. Like the victim of "Incense of the Lucky Virgin," the persona of "Soledad" could be
assigned a black identity, perhaps on the sole basis of his musical
obsession, but such specificity is probably superfluous or even irrele-
vant. This portrayal of isolation in a particular mode, exemplifying
alienation derived from social cause, addresses a syndrome of

modern America, a malady not limited to drug addicts, members of a specific race, or a particular segment of society. In fact, Hayden considered using "Soledad" as the title of the entire first section of *Words in the Mourning Time*.[6] This section notably includes "Sphinx," "Mystery Boy," "The Broken Dark," "Soledad," and "The Mirages" (*WMT*, 16), another brief study of human isolation in which a "stranger" acknowledges that he often knowingly followed mirages, just to be "less lonely then."

## Places

By strict categorical definition, few entirely new poems in either *Words in the Mourning Time* or *The Night-Blooming Cereus* focus on locale as a significant basis for subject or theme. Perhaps only "Kodachromes of the Island" (*WMT*, 27–29), Hayden's recollected impressions of a Mexican island, the atmosphere of which he distilled through drastic revision into a rare form of bone-lean exoticism, could be classified a "pure" place poem. "A Plague of Starlings" (*WMT*, 63–64) is set on the Fisk University campus, and "Smelt Fishing" (*N-BC*, 12) inherently implies a specific locale (the shores of Lake Superior), but neither of these intriguing poems, in the portrayal of ironic confrontations between man and nature or in the respective considerations of life force and spirit, calls attention to locale in the poetic process. But, of course, neither does Hayden's ultimate place poem, except that the entire country, if not the world, serves as the implicit setting of "Words in the Mourning Time" (*WMT*, 41–51), a cathartic prayer for relief from that period of slain national leaders, destructive violence in the nation's cities, and a brutalizing war fought far from home. In "Words" Hayden mourns not just for America but for "Our world / this violent ghetto."

He articulates his personal grief, cites the national dilemma, and seeks to arouse universal moral concern with a structural organization composed of ten discrete poetic units.[7] Many of the ten poems address a specific event or situation and consider moral implications, while the sequential ordering of these sections forms a progression that incorporates the thematic unity of the entire work. In the introductory segment, Hayden declares his grief for the recently

slain Martin Luther King, Jr., and Robert Kennedy, leaders
"destroyed by those they could not save." The poet regards their
murders as symptoms of the evil of the age; accordingly, his grief extends to mourn "for America, self-destructive, self-betrayed." As if
in direct response to this personal sorrow, he establishes the central
theme of the whole poem: forsaking grief as a form of vanity, he instead adopts the spiritual perspective of his Baha'i belief that the
present period of national agony and worldwide disorder is a stage
in a larger harrowing process, the "major means whereby, / oh
dreadfully, our humanness must be achieved."

Subsequent sections document the horrors of the age and thus
depict "the mourning time," yet these narrative units also provide
the "words" that describe the spiritual process, that agonizing progression toward "a human world where godliness / is possible and
man / is . . . permitted to be man." Hayden devotes the next three
poems to the war in Vietnam, noting the perverse paradox of killing
a people to "save" them, describing the war in chilling impressionistic detail (in the form of a bloody specter who "comes to my
table" from the evening television-news coverage) and envisioning
common denominators of brutality and death among the war's victims, from Vietnamese children to his former students. In Section V
he summarizes this "local" horror while expanding its scope to view
the entire world as a "violent ghetto" where an illogical, self-
destructive morality prevails:

> We hate kill destroy
> in the name of human good
> our killing and our hate destroy.

To bring this message "home" in an almost literal sense, Hayden
in another brief poem treats the insane self-destruction of urban
violence. He first personifies "Lord Riot," whom he then pictures
running amok as the "cannibal ruler / of anger's / carousals."
Equating forms of homage to this dictator with fear and destruction
("terror / his tribute / shriek of bloody glass / his praise"), Hayden
in tone and format also captures the irrational festive spirit that
often accompanies rioting and looting, with his technique of in-
terspersing through the seemingly disjointed narrative the repetition of nonsense verse ("sing hey nonny no . . . sing hey nonny
no"). Additionally, the overall effect of the "Lord Riot" poem

derives emphasis from its appearance on the page, as the poet strews words and phrases in apparent chaotic confusion, visibly suggesting the shattered fragments of disorder.

The following section contrasts sharply in its subject, sense, and formal structure because it is about Martin Luther King, Jr., and dedicated to the principles of love, nonviolence, and self-discipline. In this *"voice in the wilderness"* segment Hayden focuses the spiritual vision only glimpsed at the poem's outset. The "voice" can be "heard" at multiple levels: as a private spiritual message to the poet, delivered to him through the saving grace of the Baha'i martyr or as Hayden's own interior monologue to remind himself of what he believes, to strengthen that belief, or as the narrator's direct address to the reader. In all instances, the message is the same—only human love can mitigate the force of hatred and despair. As demanding as it will be, we must adopt the "rigorous laws of risk" and "master now love's instruments." Hayden's use of regular, orderly line lengths and stanzaic patterns in this "voice" section is in appropriate harmony with its advocacy of self-disciplined love. Although he does not mention Dr. King directly, Hayden memorializes that modern martyr with the poem's confluence of structure and moral.

In the next segment he indirectly acknowledges the difficulty, and yet maintains the possibility of sustaining love even while being hated, reviled, and persecuted. He does so with the symbolic compression derived from imagery and allusion, applying these techniques to a representation of the struggle of his race through its history of oppression and denial. Implicitly returning to the scene of the flaming ghetto, Hayden portrays a single individual who symbolizes all blacks in being "invisible man / and black boy and native / son and the / man who / lives underground whose / name nobody / knows."[8] Visible in the "light and the / distortions of light," this "fire-focused image" is thus profiled by the flames of anger and the dawn of a "zenith-time." Ultimately, Hayden's point is that if anyone can relate to the notion of enduring through a period of hatred and horror, can choose now between angry reprisal or a disciplined reliance upon faith and love, it is the archetypal black, who has for centuries been "running through / holocaust / seeking the / soul-country of his / meaning."

Once more returning to his obsessive topic, Hayden directly moralizes on the Vietnam experience:

> We must not be frightened nor cajoled
> into accepting evil as deliverance from evil.
> We must go on struggling to be human.

And he concludes "Words in the Mourning Time" by recapitulating the primary theme, the redemptive assertion that the present evil can, indeed, must be viewed, and thus endured, as the painful requisite for a vision of a better world. Hayden once more articulates this theme in bearing witness to the central Baha'i prophecy of such a harrowing progression. The experience of Baha'u'llah, as "logos, poet, cosmic hero, surgeon, architect / of our hope of peace," represents for Hayden the spiritual precedent exemplifying the agony mankind must endure en route to that new age of human harmony so fervently desired. In this faith the poet proclaims his belief that "toward him our history in its disastrous quest / for meaning is impelled." Although expressive of his personal grief, "Words in the Mourning Time" at least temporarily accomplishes what its poet bears witness to; in purging his own grief, Hayden does

> renew the vision of
> a human world where godliness
> is possible and man
> is neither gook nigger honkey wop kike
> but man
>          permitted to be man.

# Heritage

Robert Hayden could well have subtitled his "Words in the Mourning Time" something like "The Martyr's Time." Had he done so, he no doubt would have included in his coverage another martyr of that period, because the phrase "the martyr's time" originated with Malcolm X, the subject of another of Hayden's striking portraits in the category of black-heritage poems. Significantly, Hayden titled this biographical poem "El-Hajj Malik El-Shabazz" (*WMT*, 37–40) after Malcolm's ultimate identity, the name he adopted after his "hejira / to his final metamorphosis," when he renounced his secular affiliation with the Black Muslim movement in spiritual allegiance to a "raceless" Allah. This transition was for Hayden crucial, since it made Malcolm X spiritually significant, rather than just politically important. This perspective underlies the poem's title, the subordination of its subtitle "(Malcolm X)," and its epigraphical emphasis on identity and transfiguration ("*O masks and metamorphoses of Ahab, Native Son*").

Evidently keying his chronological coverage of Malcolm's life to *The Autobiography of Malcolm X,* Hayden poetically summarizes those key events and identities outlined by the subject himself in his dictation to Alex Haley.[9] In fact, he punctuates his narrative with the same identities Haley used as chapter titles, such as "Home Boy," "Detroit Red," and "Satan." As implied by this emphasis, Hayden depicts Malcolm's life as an identity quest with a spiritually significant culmination:

> As Home Boy, as Dee-troit Red,
> he fled his name, became the quarry of
> his own obsessed pursuit.

Included in that pursuit, and Hayden's coverage, is the "false dawn of vision," Malcolm's prison conversion to the racist theology of Elijah Muhammad's Nation of Islam. The poet suggests the falseness of this identity and its effect upon Malcolm through reference to moral inconsistency. Malcolm, the converted "Native Son," combats the oppression of his race while wearing the self-deceiving mask of false righteousness. As he progressed from personal self-redemption to exhorting self-pride among his black audiences, Malcolm "X'd his name, became his people's anger." He became "their scourger who / would shame them, drive them from / the lush ice gardens of their servitude." Yet in his hatred of "white-faced treachery," Malcolm "could not cleanse / [himself] of the odors of the pit." The moral paradox of this false identity was that in "rejecting Ahab, he was of Ahab's tribe." Pursuing truth while himself in a state of delusion, Malcolm, like Melville's obsessed Ahab, himself becomes diabolical in his attack upon the evils besetting his race.

For a period, the violent events of "the mourning time" seemed to bear out Malcolm's prophecies of destruction for the oppressors. But of course such violence took its toll on the oppressed as well;

Malcolm called that period "the martyr's time," acknowledging in his Black Muslim faith those "ironic trophies" the poet calls "the fruit of neo-Islam." Thereafter, in Hayden's succinct documentation, Malcolm unexpectedly strikes through his own mask with "the ebb time pilgrimage / toward revelation, hejira to / his final metamorphosis." Malcolm's trip to Mecca in 1964 opens his eyes to the raceless universality of orthodox Islam and alters his zeal from "prideful anger" to spiritual transcendence. Transformed by the experience, newly self-identified by his Sunni Muslim name, El Hajj Malik El-Shabazz, he returns to America "renewed" and "renamed," where he "became / much more than there was time for him to be." Hayden's account thus traces the evolving spiritual identity of his subject and emphasizes the tragically abrupt end of that evolution. From the poet's perspective, Malcolm X recognized at last the spiritual unity of all men, but like the other martyrs of that age, he was "destroyed by those [he] could not save."[10]

Another heritage poem, similar to the Malcolm X portrait in its thematic treatment of time as a barrier to human realization, diverges widely in poetic format and historical context. For "The Dream" (*WMT*, 12–13) Hayden uses interior narration in conjunction with an epistolary premise to dramatize the aspirations for freedom among a generation of Civil War–era blacks. He establishes a central persona in the opening section and then alternates units expressive of her thoughts and feelings with facsimile excerpts of letters written home from battle zones by her soldier son. The poet thus indirectly but dramatically represents the psychological and pragmatic perspectives of these symbolic historical characters.

The dream of the title is Sinda's vision of freedom in her particular terms, a glorious emancipation won by the heroic deeds of her lost husband and faraway sons, whom she idealizes as

> the great big soldiers marching out of gunburst,
> their faces those of Cal and Joe
> and Charlie sold to the ricefields oh sold away
> a-many and a-many a long year ago.

Sinda, old, ailing, and sensing "the ending of her dream," prays "that death, grown fretful and impatient, nagging her, / would wait a little longer, would let her see." Hayden stretches out her life and organically delays the fulfillment of her dream vision by interrupting her narrative with those excerpts from Cal's letter. The letter, as mundane reality, thus intrudes upon, contrasts with, and, in effect, thwarts Sinda's illusive dream.

Skillfully reproducing dialect and contemporary colloquialism, Hayden fills Cal's letter with detail that evokes the common soldier's boredom and anxiety between battles. He also designs its content to heighten irony of situation (the letter reveals, for example, that Cal has no inkling of Sinda's illness; he also thinks Joe is still home with her). Verbal echoes between Sinda's interior narrative and the content of Cal's letter ironically counterpoint the drama of Hayden's poem: Sinda's failing grasp on life is offset by Cal's unlettered fatalism ("no need in Dying till you die I all ways figger"). The scene of her struggle (Sinda crossed / the wavering yard, reached / a redbud tree in bloom, could go no farther, clung / to the bole") counters the scene of his combat ("this mus of been a real nice place befor the / fighting uglied it all up the judas trees is blosommed out / so pretty"). Cal describes the scene as "Almos like something you mite dream about."

Cal's letter closes with a wish for the homecoming and the reunion that the reader knows would fulfill Sinda's dream. In concluding the poem by leaving his safe return uncertain and Sinda's death imminent, Hayden compounds the irony, which strengthens both characterization and dramatic effect. The counterplay of glorious dream wish on one hand and the reality of "cold rain and / mirey mud a heap" on the other effects a plausible yet powerful statement. Sinda dies without realizing her dream, but she dies with her dream intact. The poignant drama of that situation speaks volumes about the slave-era aspirations for freedom by Hayden's forebears, as the poet reprises another page in his cultural heritage.

## Transcendence

In the personally troubling times of the late 1960s and early 1970s, Robert Hayden more and more turned or returned to the contemplation of art and nature, finding solace in the beauty of light and color, and relentlessly questing after permanent and thus transcendent meaning to allay the violent other realities of the era.

His pleasure in such works as Monet's impressionistic *Waterlilies*, and his rumination on the value and permanence of art, applied specifically on one occasion to Whistler's Peacock Room, now in the Freer Gallery of the Smithsonian Institution, exemplify those themes and that quest.

During a time of external turmoil and personal distress, the poet finds comfort in great art, typified for him by "the serene great picture that I love" and expressed in his poem "Monet's 'Waterlilies' " (*WMT*, 55). Beyond comfort and sensual gratification, Hayden also always seeks truth, and he sees in art a reflection of permanent reality. Monet's painting can provide momentary reprieve from the horrors of the age, yet its beauty also reminds him of unachieved or lost ideals. Hayden appropriately conveys these sentiments in the metaphors of light:

> The seen, the known
> dissolve in irridescence, become
> illusive flesh of light
> that was not, was, forever is.

Hayden's concluding stanza makes clear that his attachment to Monet's painting and his own creation of such bright verbal images are not mere escapism. That "flesh of light" is viewed "as through refracting tears," reminding him "of that world / each of us has lost." Speaking of *Waterlilies* to generalize about the value of art, Hayden once said that "that particular Monet helps me to recapture something—to remember something. I would say that one of the valuable functions of all the arts is to make us aware, to illuminate human experience, to make us more conscious, more alive. That's why they give us pleasure, even when their subjects or themes are 'unpleasant.' "[11]

Hayden's contemplation of art, permanence, and loss in "The Peacock Room" (*N-BC*, 10–11) illustrates well that statement. Here he is influenced by the strong emotional associations that link the history of the room's artwork, recollections of his cherished, recently deceased friend Betsy Reyneau, and inevitable intimations of his own mortality. To begin, he raises age-old fundamental questions about the relationship between art and life. Given that "Ars Longa / Vita Brevis," Hayden rhetorically poses the question, Which is crueler, life for its brevity or art for its permanent reminder of that brevity? He thus locates himself in the psychological context and physical setting ("Thoughts in the Peacock Room / where briefly I shelter") which inform the poem.

Contemplating the exotic *fin-de-siècle* art of the Peacock Room, he acknowledges its seeming irrelevance in the age of "Hiroshima Watts My Lai." Yet the room, with its gilt china shelves, elegant furnishings, and golden peacocks painted on Cordova leather-covered walls, in its effete Victorian decadence, is undeniably beautiful. Its striking touches of eccentric excess provoke the poet's reverie about the room's history and its personal connotations for him. Like the sculptor's work in Shelley's "Ozymandias," Whistler's arrogant art continues to mock its original British commissioner and tortures still Whistler's displaced, and consequently deranged, rival in the design of this "satiric arabesque of gold / peacocks on a wall peacock blue."

Hayden's reverie prominently includes thoughts of his dead friend Betsy Reyneau, to whom he dedicates the poem. Memories of her brought him to the Freer Gallery in the first place to view again her portraits on exhibit there. Prior to its donation to the Smithsonian, Charles Freer had the Peacock Room installed in his Detroit mansion, where, as a friend of the Freer family, Betsy Reyneau was honored on her twelfth birthday with a party in the room. Thoughts of Betsy come rushing back to Hayden as he views the peacocks, recalls her stories about them, and mourns her recent loss. He "sees" her there, revealed by the fluttering peacock fantails. She who once was "artist, compassionate, / clear-eyed," and "belovéd friend," is now "eyeless, old—Med School / cadaver, flesh-object / pickled in formaldehyde."

The peacocks remain long after the drama of past lives has ended. Yet that drama also remains, inexplicably infused in these artifacts. Whistler's assertive genius, the rival designer driven mad by artistic jealousy, Betsy's humane joy in life—all these human elements have been superseded by art. But these lives took their individual shapes through a consuming dedication to the very thing that outlasted them. Little wonder that in these thoughts Hayden ponders, "What is art? / What is life?" The questions, like the peacocks that provoke and symbolize them, remain, answered only in mysterious possibility. Finally, even the Peacock Room itself is reduced to "Rose-leaves and ashes," overlooked by the enigmatic smile of an ancient buddha.

If the relative permanence of art heightens one's sense of his own mortality, the natural world everywhere surrounds him with similar reminders. Robert Hayden responded to those reminders in perhaps expectable emotional ways, but with unique poetic expression. He also came to a comforting reverence for nature because his romantic vision perceived in nature a spiritual immanence—admittedly hidden, but certainly there. His "skeptical faith" in this transcendent essence of life is nowhere better expressed than in the metaphorical extension of "The Night-Blooming Cereus" (N-BC, 6–8).

As in "Waterlilies" Hayden uses the imagery of light and darkness to describe mystery beyond physical comprehension. He compares in analogical manner the experience of watching the cereus plant open its flowers during darkness to the glimpsing of an ultimate reality. As the poet notes in "Traveling through Fog" (N-BC, 15), we can never see reality for what it is; the only reality available to us is the certainty of our own uncertainty ("The cloudy dark / ensphering us seems all we can / be certain of"). The poet metaphorically represents these notions in the "Night-Blooming Cereus" with the brief blossoming of a bright flower in the dark of night.

Other contrasts heighten this drama. The speaker initially emphasizes his ambivalent attitude toward life's flower ("It repelled as much / as it fascinated me"). He is intrigued by its ever-changing appearance, but also often repulsed by that appearance, which he finds snakelike or "eyeless bird head." Contrarily, his companion, whom he addresses as "my dear," sees in the plant its potential beauty, the "imminence of the bloom." Perhaps Hayden is here talking in cryptic metaphoric code about the variation between his recurrent personal pessimism and Mrs. Hayden's sustaining, optimistic view of life.[12]

However, both watchers agree to the significance of this natural phenomenon. As "moderns" somewhat self-conscious about such primitive "nature worship," they lightheartedly banter about painting themselves and dancing "in honor of / archaic mysteries," but they also sense the "rigorous design" of life's meaning in this small miracle. This awareness moves the speaker's perception from modern science to ancient consciousness and extends his contemplation toward a metaphysical scope. He alludes to recent polygraph experiments demonstrating emotional responses in plant life and realizes that the life force, proven to exist by technology, has always existed, a "tribal sentience / in the cactus, focused / energy of will."

In this established frame of reference, the watchers feel almost like voyeuristic intruders by the time they marvel at the "achieved flower." And even as "its moonlight petals were / still unfolding," they recognize the cactus flower's birth and death as one continuous natural process, emblematic of life itself. This "lunar presence, / foredoomed, already dying," in its birth / death pangs charges the air "with plangency" expressive of life's archetypal, eternal transformations. Sensing the eternality of this silent life-force lament, the speaker is himself struck dumb by the revelation. In his struggle to relate life's "voice" in human terms he judges it

> older than human
> cries, ancient as prayers
> invoking Osiris, Krishna,
> Tezcátlipóca.

The experience leaves the observers hushed with awe, cowed in their renewed reverence for life itself, here illustrated in miniature. Hayden's metaphysical cactus thus facilitates his invocation of life's awesome mystery, discernible in the transcendent metamorphoses of the accessible natural world. As the poet notes here, elsewhere and otherwise, the essence of life is change. That certainty can distress, console, or inspire those human subjects of this eternal transformational process. "The Night-Blooming Cereus" posits such possibilities and subtly acknowledges this force, and man's divergent responses to it, as the ultimate source of his spirituality. In such modes as "Cereus" Robert Hayden connects the ordinary to the extraordinary, thereby illuminating the dark mystery of life with the glow of his passionately crafted art.

# Chapter Six
# American Ascent

## A Striking Contemporary

Robert Hayden's long years of artistic faith and dedicated labor reached toward culmination with *Angle of Ascent* in 1975. This substantial volume (seventy-six poems) includes representative selections from previous publications, along with his most recent work since *The Night-Blooming Cereus*. Hayden's two-year tenure (1976–78) as Consultant in Poetry at the Library of Congress soon followed, and the poems he crafted during that interim were published as *American Journal* in 1978. Although he did not live to see in print the expanded version of *American Journal* (1982), its reprinted and original content evidences the author's singular achievement, just as all three final collections clearly demonstrate Robert Hayden's culminating importance to American letters. By his death in 1980 he had not only achieved personal and professional "angle(s) of ascent," and the long-overdue recognition of his countrymen, but had also left a canon of poetry in significant contribution to the body of modern American literature.

## Personals

Culmination seems a fitting term also for reference to Hayden's attitude toward and treatment of his personal life in his final poems. By the early 1970s he had come full circle, returning to direct address of his own biography as subject matter. These poems are still not unguarded confessional lyrics, but rather crafted summaries of personal reminiscence, family history, or career retrospection informed by current attitudes toward self and others. The difference is that the poet no longer "distances" his life; he instead documents it. Significantly, this shift in his treatment of personal heritage themes precedes the success of Alex Haley's *Roots* (1976), and the subsequent national infatuation with genealogy and cultural history among the black population and virtually everyone else.[1] Almost as a direct announcement of his intention to return to his own "roots," Hayden begins *Angle of Ascent* with "Beginnings" (*AA*, 1–5), a brief account of his unique ancestry. From "Pennsylvania gothic, / Kentucky homespun, / [to] Virginia baroque," he locates, names, and characterizes his genetic and adopted ancestors, the "Plowdens, Finns [his mother's maiden name], / Sheffeys [his father's family name], Haydens [his foster father's family name] / and Westerfields [his foster mother's maiden name]." He follows this opening catalog with four separate sketches of his elder relatives, thereby sustaining the oral tradition of their family images and his heritage.

Hayden's sense of family and identity seems strongly intact in "Beginnings," but later poems reveal that his past still haunts as well as sustains him. The content of "Names" in *American Journal* (1978, 14; 1982, 35) illustrates this aspect of his background. The speaker in this retrospective yet timely piece recalls childhood derogatory names ("Four Eyes. And worse."), which he then "feared would break my bones." And in reference to the midlife discovery that he had never been legally adopted, he announced, "When my fourth decade came, / I learned my name was not my name." Remembering then having "felt deserted, mocked," the speaker mourns the death of past possibility; now, with both sets of parents in their graves, even his birthright is left in doubt. He acknowledges this unsettling quandary by equating the anachronistic condition of his original name (Asa Bundy Sheffey) and the life he might have had with that name: "the name on the books was dead . . . like the life I might have known." But even in the intimate revelation of traumatic personal experience, Hayden refuses to succumb to sentimentalism or self-pity. He closes and saves the poem with the inherent irony of an attorney's legal judgment of his status: "You don't exist—at least / not legally, the lawyer said." The poet responds by asking what he is; how he *does* exist, "as ghost, double, or alter ego then?" Hayden in raising the question is really asking *who* he is, and, implicitly, who he might have been. In a sense, the poet answers his own rhetorical questions in the belated act of writing the poem. The passing of years allowed him the dispassionate ability to reopen this old wound, which he sealed in his final years with "Names," and by legally adopting the name he had used all his life.

In this biographical context Hayden also surveys how far he has come and how he got there, through an allegorical account of his career as an artist, in a poem he titles "For a Young Artist" (*AA*, 8-10). The title seems at first to have little to do with the content of the poem, yet it has everything to do with it; that title signals the universal application of Hayden's theme about the risks and rewards of artistic commitment. He draws his mythic content from the Gabriel Márquez story "A Very Old Man with Enormous Wings," adapting it to a symbolic rendering of his own, or any artist's, experience in an apathetic or even hostile culture.[2]

The essential story depicts a fallen flyer, "a naked old man / with bloodstained wings," whose presence and being mystify "the curious" who come to view this oddity. In the events leading up to the old man's attempt to regain flight, Hayden expresses his "real" concerns: public misunderstanding of the artist, the conflicting requisites of a life devoted to art—both vulnerability and strength, and the culminating rewards of a commitment to the loneliness of art. He allegorizes these aspects, respectively, through the failure of the crowd to comprehend the old man's language, in his nakedness and their curiosity, and with his awkward, often failing, but finally successful efforts to get airborne ("He strains, an awk- / ward patsy, sweating strains / leaping falling"). The poet also emphasizes the ambivalent attitude of society toward its artists. Not knowing whether the old man is human or fowl, but assuming his inferiority, "they spread him a pallet / in the chicken house," and offer him scraps from the table. They value him mainly as a curiosity, and charge admission to view this wonder. The paying onlookers seem roughly divided between extreme misconceptions of the artist: is he "actual angel?" or "carny freak?" Some "crossed themselves and prayed / his blessings; / [others] catcalled and chunked at him." Hayden suggests an appropriate response to such public treatment through his concluding stress on self-fulfillment, where the old man's long, hard struggle culminates in transcendent flight, with "silken rustling in the air, / the angle of ascent / achieved."

Significant alterations of Márquez's story line clarify Hayden's allegorical purpose in the poem. Whereas the Márquez character heals gradually, and remains for some years as a burden to his "keepers," who are glad to see him finally fly off, Hayden's old man works feverishly to attain flight, and his painful struggle goes unseen by the "curious" as he achieves his ascent in the solitude of darkness. Perhaps the most notable innovation is Hayden's emphasis on the old man's nakedness, a clear suggestion of his (or any artist's) exposure of his soul to an often uncaring or uncomprehending audience. Such symbolism provides insight into Hayden's personal anxieties, as it inherently rationalizes the symbolic indirection of the poem itself, but more importantly the nakedness hints that artistic flight requires such an unfettered state. Because "they could not make him hide / his nakedness" or conform to their precepts of conventionality, the artist's total commitment results in achievement true to himself and his art. Thus "To a Young Artist," while accommodating a purely mythic reading, allegorizes the poet's own experience and provides instructional inspiration for other artists.

One of Hayden's last poems brings together these personal perceptions of artistic sacrifice, alienation, and identity. This time he adopts the persona of "The Tattooed Man" (*AJ*, 82, 19–23) to "confess" private anxieties through an apt metaphorical medium. The speaker clearly yearns for human contact and love; in that unfulfilled longing he shares a certain general alienation with his audience. But his unique status as a sideshow attraction, made grotesque with numerous tattoos, further separates him from those who "gawk." Paradoxically, the features that attract general attention also repel individual, personal relationships. Those masterpieces embroidered in his skin are precious to him for their beauty and for the pain they cost ("I clenched my teeth in pain; / all art is pain / suffered and outlived"), but such "bizarrity" obviates the love he craves. The tattooed man inventories his decorations in exactly those terms—terms suggestive of Hayden's personal demons, and his poetic exorcism of them.

The speaker's tattoo patterns recurrently commingle Christian mythology and morality with sensual pagan joys: "Da Vinci's Last Supper— / a masterpiece / in jewel colors / on my breast," surrounded on his upper torso by "gryphons" and "a gaiety of imps / in cinnabar," highlighting a portrait of "naked Adam / embracing naked Eve." A black-widow spider peers from her tattooed web, which spans "belly to groin," suggesting the sexual impulse also implicit in "the birds-of-paradise / perched on my thighs." Although the speaker begins his interior monologue by decrying his alien status, wishing "to break through, / to free myself," he concludes in acceptance of both his chronic longing ("I yearn I yearn.") and his identity, whether self-made or imposed: "I cannot / (will

not?) change. / It is too late / for any change / but death. / I am I."
The tattooed man is Robert Hayden's metaphorical disguise of
himself, but the persona could assume an independent identity as
well, one that "figuratively" dramatizes the modern plight of
alienation.

Finally, all the biographical and poetic evidence suggests that
Robert Hayden's personal demons were laid to rest before he was.
Moreover, he found toward the end renewed joy and hope in the
progeny represented by his adopted grandson, Michael Ahmán
Tedla. He commits these emotions to print in "The Year of the
Child" (AJ, 82, 43–45). Speaking directly to the child who will
someday read "his poem," Hayden refers to the boy's namesakes,
in hoping the names of archangel, great poet (Michael Harper), and
"Abysinnian Ahmán, / hero of peace," will prove talismans to pro-
tect his grandson "in a world that is / no place for a child." The
poet recalls child victims around the world (Guyana, Biafra, War-
saw) in recent years, and vows a better life for Michael's generation.
Seeing this vision of hope in the boy's "brilliant eyes, whose gaze /
renews, transforms / each common thing," Hayden finds present
contentment in the joy of the moment. His benedictive closing
evokes just such a vision in its eclectic fusion of secular wish, Navaho
Indian song, and Baha'i prayer:

> May Huck and Jim
> attend you. May you walk
> with beauty before you,
> beauty behind you, all
> around you, and
> The Most Great Beauty keep
> you His concern.

Mark Twain's "Huck and Jim" represent the bond of human
brotherhood, formulated in spiritual terms by the Baha'i Faith and
universalized succinctly in the Navaho "Prayer of the Night
Chant."

Thus in his most personal poems Robert Hayden often explored
themes of identity, sought first in his ancestry and finally through
his progeny. In their singular detail these explorations are unique,
yet in their general thematic patterns they share the widespread
concerns of their times and their culture. As Ralph Ellison once

remarked about the search-for-identity theme, "It is *the* American theme."[3] Hayden *lived*, as well as eloquently expressed, that theme so central to the cultural consciousness of his generation. Such congruence makes his work undeniably relevant; and the artistic merit of the work doubles one's conviction that Robert Hayden's poetry speaks to and, in a larger sense, for the widening audience it is now beginning to find.

## People

Had Robert Hayden finished his planned poem about Josephine Baker, she would have been in the good company of notables ranging from Crispus Attucks to Paul Robeson. In such variety Hayden's final collection of character sketches displays the poet's sustained interest in dramatic portraiture and his exquisitely refined skill in this mode. Informed by psychological acuity, subtly shaded with an empathetic understanding of subjects, these profiles extend and culminate the author's pantheon of admired and intriguing people, many of them racial heroes neglected or misshaped by history or legend.

"A Letter from Phillis Wheatley" (*AJ*, 78, 1–2; *AJ*, 82, 3–4) illustrates these features, and more. Here the poet uses an epistolary technique in the creation of what he called a "psychogram," a psychological profile of this first recognized American black poet within her historical-cultural context. Ostensibly written from England to her friend Orbour Tanner in 1773, the letter derives its verisimilitude from Hayden's imitation of Wheatley's "voice" through his deft creation of vocal cadence, latinate diction, and a plausible "style."

The resultant poem abounds in irony. Its drama grows out of disparities between those ironies Wheatley notes and those that are lost on her, but not the reader. For example, she mentions the ironic contrast between her recent uneventful ocean crossing and the earlier westward crossing as a slave, but it is the reader who senses the irony in her assumption that her enslavement ("my Destined— / Voyage") was God-willed. She also sees no disparity in being received by the nobility, yet excluded from joining her hosts at supper ("I dined apart / like captive Royalty"). As a true "Patriot," she seems more concerned about the loyalty of being presented at the English court, but such a prospect is not without ironies she does perceive ("I thought of Pocahontas"). Even in "Idyllic England," she realizes, "there is / no Eden without its Serpent," yet in expectable neoclassical manner she resists "Sombreness," even in intimate correspondence. Hayden further humanizes his subject with her closing anecdote about an incident she considers "Droll." Hayden's fully dimensioned version of the "Sable Muse" displays her appreciation of life's lighter ironies also, as shown by her amusement at being asked by a blackened young British chimney sweep, "Does you, M'lady, sweep chimneys too?"

In addition to his consistent feel for human drama in the individual portraits, one can also discern a significant trend in Hayden's last "people poems." More and more he distilled them down to pure essence, saying less to mean more. The four-line sketch of "Crispus Attucks" in *Angle of Ascent* (20) perhaps begins the trend; "John Brown" (*AJ*, 82, 5–9) typifies it; and "Homage to Paul Robeson" (*AJ*, 82, 16) certainly culminates it. In the first, Hayden begins by calling Attucks a "Name in a footnote," and seemingly limits his poetic account to similar length and substance. However, the brief sketch is loaded with allusive and imagistic meaning. In visual allusion to Paul Revere's 1770 engraving of the Boston Massacre, the poet captures this black patriot, the first American to fall in the Revolution, "propped up / by bayonets, forever falling." Like the figures on Keats's Grecian urn, Attucks becomes eternally static, yet endlessly in motion. Unlike those romantic figures, however, Hayden's figure is also "caught" in the symbolic tension of being "shrouded" (in the several senses of that carefully chosen pun) by the flags of both Betsy Ross (traditional patriotism, oblivious to black history) and Marcus Garvey (black nationalistic support of a rightful place in history and geography). While no prerequisite for full appreciation of "Crispus Attucks," a glancing familiarity with Hayden's earlier, longer poem about Attucks in the 1942 Hopwood manuscript ("Whereas in Freedom's Name . . ."; 24 ll.) verifies that his latest "less" is certainly "more."[4]

The same could be said of Hayden's early and final drafts of his "Homage to Paul Robeson," except that these two versions were separated by weeks rather than years. The penultimate draft devotes ten lines to establishing a context of history and reminiscence.[5]

Subsequently, in response to the feelings behind the poem's closing perspective, "All else fades," Hayden in fact caused all else to fade by cutting and compressing the poem to its final five-line length:

> Call him deluded, say that he
> was dupe and by half-truths betrayed.
> I speak him fair in death,
> remembering the power of his
> compassionate art. All else fades.

When Hayden found this final form, he was seeking ultimate truth about the maligned subject. Of Robeson he thus wrote, "I speak him fair in death." Ironically, Hayden now in his own death continues to speak Robeson fair, through the enduring power of his own compassionate art.

## Places

Hayden yet marvels his readers because he continued to marvel at the diversity of the land of his birth. As Americans in the 1970s were looking backward at their ancestral roots and looking forward to technological advances and space exploration, Hayden's extraordinary poetic pulse kept rhythm with the heartbeat of the nation. His intrigue with technology and the space program prompted "Astronauts" (*AJ*, 78, 30–31; *AJ*, 82, 55–56), a "place poem" only in that Hayden portrays these "heroic antiheroes" as they were seen in "the mineral glare and / shadow of moonscape" on television screens across the country. The anticlimactic contrast between this otherworldly locale ("the calcined stillness / of once Absolute Otherwhere") and the incongruous blend of the astronaut's no-nonsense scientific objectivity and boyish glee ("Wow, they / exclaim; oh boy, this is it") underlines the limitation of heroes and heroic endeavor in an age adrift from the romance of the past, and technological in its future. Because the astronauts are "smaller than myth and / poignantly human," they can lift our eyes, but not our souls. Hayden speaks for his countrymen when he asks, "Why are we troubled? / What do we ask of these men? / What do we ask of ourselves?"

The poet "returns" to earthly locales of personal remembrance and regional history in two other late poems. Both seem geographically and psychically related to his earlier coverage in "Tour 5." Again, southern landscapes summon up observations on man's capacities for both evil and love. "The Dogwood Trees" (AJ, 82, 37) locates these human potentials among contrasting scenes of natural flora ("white bracts of dogwood / clustered") and unnatural violence ("shrill slums / were burning, / the crooked crosses flared"). But Robert Hayden and Robert Slagle find a bond of human daring in their "bitter knowledge / of the odds against comradeship."

Hayden retraces a similar southern route through the dramatized fiction of "Theory of Evil" (AJ, 82, 10–11). Not until mid-poem does the author parenthetically attribute the narrated legend to his own travel on the Natchez Trace, and his consequent musing "on the cussedness / of the human race." By then the reader is "hooked" on the story and becoming cognizant of its moral theme. Based on regional lore, it is a story of two totally evil, murdering thieves who preyed with incredible cruelty upon travelers along the Trace. The poem's macabre detail translates grotesque fiction into essential truth about human depravity, as it describes man's treatment of his fellow man. Hence Hayden's title.

Big Harpe and Little Harpe, the murderers, are identified also as "mystic / evil's face." Their diabolical cruelty is matched only by the vileness of their own deaths: accosting a "Po' wayfaring / stranger," "Big Harpe slashed / him open, filled / his belly with stones / then left him for / the river to eat." Brought eventually to equally cruel justice, "when Big Harpe's head / had been cut off, / they took and nailed it / to a sycamore tree." Hayden compounds his theme of man's unnatural evil with a devastating parenthetical commentary on Big Harpe's decapitated head: "(Buzzards gathered / but would not feed)." This head of evil in its afterlife "voice" fantastically expresses Hayden's dark theme:

> Almighty God
> he fashioned me
> for to be a scourge,
> the scourge of all humanity.

Finally, Hayden returns again to the inherent symbolism of natural surroundings to shed another glimpse of his ambivalent feelings toward the beyond. "The Moose Wallow" (*AA*, 19) suggests similarities in possible interpretation with Robert Frost's "Stopping by Woods on a Snowy Evening," since both speakers seem on allegorical "paths" bounded by unknown temptations and hidden dangers. Hayden imbues the unseen moose of his poem with such mysteriousness. Although the speaker's "friends warned of moose that / often came to the wallow," he ventured there anyway, both fearing and hoping to see them "in their battle crowns." In that locale, he feels "their presence / in the dark" as "hidden watchers." With this cryptic allegory the poet suggests his mixed emotions about whether the other side of life holds revelation or annihilation. Yet by designating the moose "hidden watchers," he assigns them a spiritual presence and implies an assumption of life's purpose, regardless of personal destiny. Like some of the other "places" he describes, "The Moose Wallow" for Robert Hayden is another point of departure in the poetic contemplation of ultimate truths beyond place or time.

## Heritage

Discussion in this chapter of Hayden's last poems about people has been limited by space, but also by design. Because he merged almost without exception his final character portraits and his concluding address of personal and racial heritage, one can illuminate the latter with preliminary reference to some of the former.[6] For example, "Free Fantasia: Tiger Flowers" (*AA*, 6–7) as much animates the cultural milieu of Paradise Valley during an earlier era as it personifies Tiger Flowers, the boxer–racial hero–"elegant avenger." Also both internally and externally indicative of the poet's return to his roots is his resurrection and reprinting of a "memory poem" after letting it "steep" for almost thirty years. "Double Feature" (*AJ*, 82, 36) in only slightly different form was first published in 1950.[7] It too presents a slice of Paradise Valley life, recalled in fond detail and bittersweet memory by the man who was that boy who attended those movies at the Dunbar Theater.

But the *magnum opus* of the genre is "Elegies for Paradise Valley" (*AJ*, 78, 4–13; *AJ*, 82, 25–34), a collection of eight poems evocative of Hayden's personal past and cultural heritage. Narrated

in first-person intimacy throughout, these poems tell much about
Paradise Valley and perhaps more about Robert Hayden. The first
two of these document the horrors of ghetto life (prejudice, drug
addiction, death) to which even the young children were exposed,
and from which "Godfearing / elders, even Godless grifters" tried
in vain to shelter them. Reference to the elders leads into successive
discrete poetic units devoted to specific personages, and the
"Elegies" become more recognizable as such. Section Three
eulogizes "Uncle Henry / (murdered Uncle Crip)" at the
remembered scene of his wake. Picturing Crip's coffin "in the front
room where / the Christmas tree had stood," Hayden's recall of the
neighbors' compliments on the coffin ("Beautiful. . . . Is it
mahogany?") prompts an associative reverie of Uncle Crip's love of
the Bert Williams "talk-sing" rendition of "Mahogany," and
Crip's joyous laughter at his young nephew's naive response to the
song. Such reverie transcends mere nostalgia; it also exemplifies
Hayden's ability to create and dramatize character without the
character's active presence in the poem. From the "event" of Crip's
wake, to the recall of his person, to a dramatized portrait of his
character, Crip comes alive, at first in Hayden's memory and now in
the poem.

The poet recalls another character by putting an ironically appropriate question to the long-dead neighborhood fortune-teller:
"Whom now do you guide, Madame Artelia?" Causing her also to
"materialize before the eye / of memory," he describes that vision
of "AfroIndian features," "Gypsy dress," "silver crucifix / and
manycolored beads." He locates Madame Artelia in her
"waitingroom," and recalls a séance there attended by "Ma" (Sue
Hayden) and "Auntie" (Aunt Roxie). Hayden, as a young boy, got
only as far as that remembered waiting room; the account of the
séance derives from conversation overheard later. Apparently
Madame Artelia provided spiritual communion with dead Uncle
Crip to the satisfaction of at least one of the two women: "She went
into a trance, / Auntie said afterward. . . . And Crip came." The
"voice" of Crip affords them the comfort they paid for at Artelia's
door: "dying's not death. Do not grieve." With their divergent
responses to the experience Hayden subtly characterizes his foster
mother and aunt: "Auntie began to cry / and poured herself a glass
of gin. / Didn't sound a bit like Crip, Ma snapped." Typifying
Hayden's reminiscent mode and dramatic purpose, this ostensible

portrait of one character (Madame Artelia) gives way to a recalled episode, which in turn characterizes two more people prominent in the author's personal heritage.

Hayden picks up the "where are you now?" opening of the Madame Artelia poem as the rhetorical basis for his next poem, an *ubi sunt* inventory of past characters, a "Paradise Valley Anthology" of sorts. He implicitly divides the poem into two sections, listing women in the first and men at the end. The females range from young "stagestruck Nora" to "snuffdipping Lucy, who played us 'chunes' on her guitar," but all have in common their unknown and unknowable destinies. As Hayden's poignant refrain acknowledges, "Let vanished rooms, let dead streets tell." The collection of men is more numerous and more dispiriting. Perhaps Hayden simply encountered more of such characters on the ghetto streets as a youngster; perhaps some were contemporary acquaintances. In any event, their separate natures ("defeated," "shell-shocked," "taunted," "cursing," "dopefiend") make the repeated questioning of their present whereabouts truly rhetorical. The entire catalog projects a dark theme of thwarted aspiration, early and violent death, cynical disillusionment, and tragic waste.

In recognition of this mood, its creator deliberately moderates it to introduce Section Six, balancing his thoughts "Of death. Of loving too." And he returns to Uncle Crip for that balance. Crip is introduced into the poem by recollection of his death, but his more important function is as the symbol of love and joy. In this unit the poet introduces the subject of his youthful ambivalence about oppositions of death and love, sin and salvation, and joy in life versus life as a vale of righteous tears. He subtly evokes these dichotomies with his remembered joyful response to "sinful" music like Jellyroll Morton's "brimstone / piano on the phonograph." Only the "sinful hymned" such music, "while the churchfolk loured."[8] Caught in the middle, the young boy longed for love: "I scrounged for crumbs: / I yearned to touch the choirlady's hair." But such familiar physical contact was as out of place in church as it was taboo in the strict religious morality imposed upon his psyche. In direct contrast to the untouchable symbolic choirlady is Uncle Crip: "I wanted Uncle Crip / to kiss me, but he danced / with me instead." Hayden still recalls Crip as love and death, remembering how they "Balled-the-Jack" in deliciously forbidden joy, "laughing, shaking the gasolier / a later stillness dimmed [by Crip's death]."

The next poem, about the Gypsy population of Paradise Valley, diverts the reader's attention from Hayden, but both Crip and his thematic function remain. In illustrating the black residents' superstitious prejudice against the Gypsies among them, Hayden notes the irony of the black minority, oppressed by ignorant prejudice, viewing another minority the same way on the same basis. But it is Uncle Crip who articulates the real moral equation. Observing Gypsy behavior in a funeral procession for their dead "king," he sums it up: "They take on bad as Colored Folks, / Uncle Crip allowed. Die like us too." Hayden, having learned that lesson as a boy from his uncle, concludes the poem about the Gypsies by calling them "aliens among the alien . . . like us like us." Just as Crip symbolizes joy in life, he too is the agency of the perception that Gypsies and blacks have a common bond based on more than being fellow victims of prejudice, on more than similar conditions of social existence. It is the bond of a shared enduring spirit and unquenchable vitality that Crip recognizes in, and Hayden attributes to, both his race and those alien "pornographers of gaudy otherness."

For the final "elegy," Hayden returns, like a moth to a flame, more explicitly to Crip and the theme of that conflict within his own psyche. Now shown clearly through the righteous eyes of the "old Christians" to be an unrepentant sinner, Uncle Crip fully personifies Hayden's youthful dilemma. Crip represents joy and love and warmth, yet he also means sin and damnation. A cultural and emotional captive of hidebound Christian morality, yet longing for more than sterile righteousness, Hayden remembers himself as a young "performer," dancing with Crip, speaking his memorized pieces in Sunday School, and hiding his longing and guilt from both. But he could not hide from himself: "I knew myself (precocious / in the ways of guilt / and secret pain) / the devil's own rag babydoll."

In such revelation and through the symbolic presence of Uncle Crip, "Elegies" is ultimately a personal poem rather than a cultural document. Hayden forthrightly describes his early (and continuing) struggle to reconcile these two opposed forces, one a natural instinct, the other a cultural behavior ingrained in his personality. In a sense, the poem could be regarded as Hayden's declaration of self-emancipation. By paying homage to Uncle Crip's side of the opposition, he somehow compensates for resisting for so long his own impulse toward joy. In the stricter sense of his title, while he mourns in elegiac reverie Crip and the others, he also laments his own loss of what he deprived himself of during those intervening years.

Psychoanalytic speculation aside, the set of Paradise Valley poems represents also an aesthetically satisfying artistic achievement, because the personal lyric is woven through a rich cultural tapestry and because the diverse characters come to life, making the poet's confessional response to them believable and justified. "Elegies for Paradise Valley" thus interweaves black heritage, dramatized character portrayal, and personal expression of psychological revelation. By the close of his career these prominent features of Robert Hayden's poetry came together within individual poems, completing a final step in the evolution of his distinct poetic voice.

## American Poet

When the "People's Poet" of Depression-era Detroit was asked in 1976 to author another Phi Beta Kappa poem for the Ann Arbor chapter, he took the occasion of America's bicentennial year to compose his "American Journal" (*AJ*, 78, 32–37;( *AJ*, 82, 57–62), a daring attempt to capture in poetry what the nation is in essence. He presents his country and its people in the perceptions of an alien being from another galaxy and a culture far advanced. Such a premise would at first seem ideally suited to an objective assessment of America and Americans, but the scientific scrutiny of the narrator–journal keeper in fact accommodates an "insider's" view, highlighted by innate ironies, and the increasingly evident emotional attachment of the speaker for those he would catalog, dissect, and analyze. This "affect," intensely experienced and grudgingly recorded by the alien speaker, conveys the essential point of the poem—the expression of what constitutes the essence of America. Even the most remote outsider cannot remain an outsider in this country, cannot resist the emotional response (both attraction and repulsion) to the totality of what is America. That phenomenon of feeling is Hayden's implicit conclusion as to the essence of what America is, the one central characteristic of an otherwise diverse, seemingly chaotic amalgam.

The poet subtly draws this conclusion through the use of an in-

novative format, sectioning the poem into fourteen separate entries
in the alien's "American Journal." It is a curious mix of informal,
impressionistic diary style and detached scientific record. The
analyst's concern for objectivity is belied by the emotional implications of that concern. He worries that his supervisors will find fault
with his work and will be scrutinizing his reports for lapses in
analytical methodology. By reading the journal entries in much the
same way for a completely different purpose, one discerns Hayden's
technique and discovers "his" America.

The "Journal" begins with a straightforward statement of the
task facing the alien (and the poet). Among "this baffling / multi
people" of "extremes and variegations," and "almost frightening
/ energy," the observer ponders how he can "best describe these
aliens in my / reports." His reference to "aliens" initiates the recurrent irony afforded by Hayden's chosen perspective, just as the first
entry establishes the need for a method for analyzing and summarizing "the americans." The next report reveals that he (it?) in-
filtrates the species by adopting at will any of the diverse human
variants encountered. This adaptation includes "their varied
pigmentations," which the analyst judges "the imprecise and
strangering / distinctions by which they live  by which they / justify
their cruelties to one another."

Not surprisingly, he finds Americans primitive by his standards.
But as he labels them "charming savages" and "enlightened
primitives," one begins to sense the encroaching emotional involvement, even when he notes his subjects' arrogant pride in their
national identity while in their total ignorance of "other beings / in
the universe." The alien later catalogs their technological advances
("a veritable populace / of machines . . . foot prints on the
moon"), but again reduces them accurately to paradox ("a
wastefully ingenious / people").

With the next entry a pattern of response emerges, one that
repeats itself through the journal. The investigator will begin with
notation of objective inventory, then be betrayed by an emotional
association or response to his facts, and conclude in confession of his
emotions. For example, his listing of geographic features ("oceans
deserts mountains . . .") gives way to "vistas reminding me of /
home," followed shortly by acknowledgment of ambivalent but
strong feelings:

despite
the tension i breathe in i am attracted to
the vigorous americans          disturbing sensuous
appeal of so many          never to be admitted


On the subject of "something they call the american dream," the reporter for the first time includes in his journal samples of the native language of those Americans asked about that dream. Here Hayden employs his sensitivity to the social connotations of idiom in displaying a spectrum of colloquialisms expressive of diverse cultural values. The "narrator" simply records these opinions in direct quotation. Ironically, with all his scientific intellect, he understands little except that people are beginning to notice his "funny accent," so he must "learn to use okay / their pass word."

The timing of the alien's expedition brings him into contact with Americans during the protest demonstrations of the late 1960s and the bicentennial celebration of 1976. Again, close physical contact with these earthlings both attracts and repulses him. Similar paradoxical principles govern his conclusions about dissent and hypocrisy among Americans. He perceives the inconsistencies in American values but is blind to the shortcomings of his own culture. Of dissent and protest he reports, "The Counselors / would silence them"; of bicentennial patriotism, "much grandiloquence much buying and selling." With the stilted mechanical voice of his narrator expressing such disparaties, Hayden balances his own objectivity: He reminds those who protest of the past sacrifices, which ensure their freedom to do so ("a past few understand / and many scorn"), yet he also refuses to "sanction / old hypocrisies" with false spectacle and banal symbols ("blonde miss teen age / america waving from a red white and blue flower / float as the goddess of liberty").

Late entries revive the alien's themes of investigative mode and fear of failure in his task. Although the journal-keeper easily impersonates Americans in their variousness ("bankers grey afro and dashiki long hair and jeans / hard hat yarmulka mini skirt"), he still cannot reduce that variety to scientific quantification. His summation of this dilemma also functions as Hayden's perception of the nation he has passionately observed as a truth-seeking artist:

america    as much a problem in metaphysics as
it is a nation earthly entity an iota in our
galaxy    an organism that changes even as i
examine it    fact and fantasy never twice the
same    so many variables

By the end the alien is devoting entire diary entries to his attraction to the Americans. Although he can never admit it to his own kind, and although he doubts he could exist among Americans for long ("psychic demands far too severe"), he still is drawn to "their variousness their ingenuity / their elan vital  and that some thing  essence / quiddity  i cannot penetrate or name." His final frustration again suggests Robert Hayden's ultimate point: that "essence" is the very phenomenon experienced by the puzzled alien. That totally objective scientist cannot avoid being caught up in the American experience. This resistance to scientific analysis, this need to respond subjectively to America, is what America is.

On another psychological level, "American Journal" is about Robert Hayden's own relationship to the country and its people. At this level the journal-keeper is a persona masking the poet's identity and "objectifying" his voice in expression of passionate response. The persona's experience in many ways parallels Hayden's efforts to cope with what he found both good and bad about America. As a poet (albeit one "with enormous wings") he also was to a certain extent "alien," and yet an acute observer of his fellow man. He took great comfort in that which he judged noble, virtuous, and humane among his kind but was horrified by the ugliness, violence, and evil observable in the same group of people. Hence, the alien's supposedly scientific findings, which are clearly subjective and emotional, are also the perceptions and responses of Robert Hayden.

As a black poet Hayden had to resist the temptations to "pass": first, to "pass" by conforming his poetry to standards of white prejudice or black chauvinism; second, as an individual, to "pass" in the sense of conforming to what was respectable and acceptable in his personal life. He never wavered in his resolve or practice of artistic integrity, refusing to be propagandist or apologist for any point of view but his own. For a long time he chose to keep his personal psychology out of his poetry; then he carefully objectified his personal feelings in all but the most autobiographically intense poems. Finally, with such works as "Elegies for Paradise Valley" and "American Journal," he fully integrated his life and his art. This struggle for objectivity is reflected in the intense emotional responses recorded by the alien journal-keeper, but even in that allegory Hayden artfully distances the reporting of his own emotions by converting them to an alien's response.

Perhaps the ultimate irony of Robert Hayden's life and art is that this "alien," this "minority" in race, in unique family background, in religious denomination, in "ivory tower" profession, and in lonely artistic calling, for all his singularity, was one of the most sensitively astute and expansive chroniclers of modern American history and culture. His themes are *the* American themes; his artistry in expression of them should put him in the first rank of contemporary American poets. The same history for which he had such a great respect will in time return that respect in full measure.

# Notes and References

## Chapter One

1. Sources for the subsequent biographical information about Robert Hayden's early years include published interviews by Paul McCluskey in *How I Write / 1* (New York, 1972), pp. 133–212; John O'Brien in *Interviews with Black Writers* (New York, 1973), pp. 108–23; Richard Layman in *Conversations with Writers* (Detroit, 1977), 1:156–79; an interview by Dennis Gendron in his doctoral dissertation, "Robert Hayden: A View of His Life and Development as a Poet" (University of North Carolina, 1975), pp. 152–234; and my own unpublished conversations with Hayden conducted most recently in Washington, D.C., on March 9 and September 18, 1977; in Annapolis, Maryland, on April 18, 1978; in New York on December 15, 1979; and in Ann Arbor, Michigan, on February 24, 1980. Henceforth, a single specific source will be cited only when the information is attributable to that source alone; otherwise, the reader may assume that Hayden touched on a given subject with more than one of the above interviewers, including myself.

2. Hayden obliquely alludes to these circumstances and events in his recent poem "Names," which appears in *American Journal* (Taunton, Mass., 1978), and most recently in *American Journal* (New York, 1982).

3. McCluskey, *How I Write*, p. 142.

4. Layman, *Conversations*, pp. 160–61.

5. McCluskey, *How I Write*, p. 140.

6. Fetrow, New York interview, December 15, 1979.

7. Gendron, "Robert Hayden," p. 177.

8. By then his natural mother was remarried to Albert Moore, whom Hayden admired enough to employ his name as part of the pseudonym ("Christopher Albert Moore") he used when submitting his poems in the 1938 Hopwood competition (New York interview, December 15, 1979).

9. Fetrow, New York interview, December 15, 1979.

10. According to Hayden, he was also a "re-write man" who wrote headlines as well (Gendron, "Robert Hayden," p. 42 n.).

11. Hayden claimed not to have a copy of the play himself, and since no one else is familiar with it, what we know about the drama is limited to what Hayden somewhat reluctantly revealed.

12. Layman, *Conversations*, p. 162.

13. *The Negro Caravan*, ed. Sterling A. Brown, Arthur P. Davis, and Ulysses Lee (New York, 1941), pp. 404–8.

14. Layman, *Conversations*, p. 165.

15. McCluskey, *How I Write*, p. 175.

16. This information appears as a note prefacing the table of contents and the content of the 1942 Hopwood manuscript.

17. Because Hayden left Wayne State without having completed the technical requirements for the bachelor's degree (the degree was withheld because of a deficiency in a geometry course), a portion of his work taken as a student of "advanced standing" at the University of Michigan was applied toward his B.A. degree from Wayne State University.

18. For a more complete account of Hayden's relationship with Auden, especially in later years, see Layman's interview, p. 166.

19. McCluskey, *How I Write*, pp. 169–80.

20. Ibid., pp. 157–61.

21. Layman, *Conversations*, p. 168.

22. Selden Rodman, "Negro Poets," *New York Times Book Review* (October 10, 1948), p. 27.

23. McCluskey, *How I Write*, p. 203.

24. Ibid., p. 188.

25. Layman, *Conversations*, p. 174.

26. The Heritage Series presently includes volumes by such notable black poets as Ishmael Reed, Arna Bontemps, Frank Horne, Dudley Randall, Owen Dodson, Ray Durem, and James Thompson.

27. Quoted from Pool's "Robert Hayden: Poet Laureate" in *Negro Digest* 15 (June 1966):41.

28. "Three Recent Volumes," *Poetry* 110 (July 1967): 268.

29. *World Order* 5 (Spring 1971):33.

30. "For a world where a man is a man, a poet a poet," *New York Times Book Review*, January 24, 1971, pp. 4–5, 22.

31. *Afro-American Literature; An Introduction*, ed. Hayden, David J. Burrows, and Frederick R. Lapides (New York, 1971). For Hayden's acknowledgment of, and intention to represent, poetic views of the ongoing controversy over the Afro-American poet's proper function, see pp. 103–4.

32. O'Brien, *Interviews*, pp. 108–23.

33. Charles T. Davis, "Robert Hayden's Use of History," in *Modern Black Poets*, ed. Donald B. Gibson (Englewood Cliffs, N.J.: Prentice-Hall, 1973), pp. 96–111. See also Fetrow, "Robert Hayden's 'Frederick Douglass': Form and Meaning in a Modern Sonnet," *CLA Journal* 17 (September 1973):79–84, and Maurice J. O'Sullivan, Jr., "The Mask of Allusion in Robert Hayden's 'The Diver,' " *CLA Journal* 17 (September 1973): 85–92.

34. The material in those two issues was subsequently reprinted as

*Chant of Saints*, ed. Michael S. Harper and Robert B. Stepto (Urbana, 1979). This anthology of Afro-American literature, art, and scholarship, in scope and perspective, rivals in its own age the critical importance of Alain Locke's *The New Negro* in 1925.

35. Fetrow, Ann Arbor interview, February 24, 1980.

*Chapter Two*

1. From *Heart-Shape in the Dust*, p. 28. Subsequent quotations from this volume will be documented within the text by page numbers. A similar documentation system for quoted material from other collections will be used in subsequent chapters, using title abbreviations and page-number references.

2. See David Galler, "Three Recent Volumes," *Poetry* 110 (1967): 268, and David Littlejohn, *Black on White* (New York, 1966), p. 86.

3. For an interview discussion of "A Ballad of Remembrance," see *How I Write*, pp. 157–61.

4. See also Countee Cullen's "The Black Christ" in *The Black Christ* (New York: Harper & Brothers, 1929), p. 69.

5. Langston Hughes, "Song for a Dark Girl" from *Fine Clothes to the Jew* (New York: Alfred A. Knopf, 1927), p. 75.

6. Arna Bontemps, "From the Dark Tower" from *Copper Sun* (New York: Harper & Brothers, 1927), p. 3. Since Bontemps's poem appeared in Cullen's *Caroling Dusk* in 1927, it definitely predates Hayden's. "A Black Man Talks of Reaping" is reprinted in *Negro Caravan*, p. 381.

7. Hughes's poem first appeared in *A New Song* (New York: International Workers Order, 1938), and is reprinted in *Negro Caravan*, pp. 370–72.

8. For other poetic treatments of this theme, see James Weldon Johnson's "White Witch" (1917) in *The Book of American Negro Poetry*, ed. Johnson (New York: Harcourt, Brace, & Co., 1922), p. 120, and Hughes's "Silhouette" in *One-Way Ticket* (New York: Knopf, 1949), p. 56.

9. For an example of effective irony of this kind where Hayden subtly lets the lynchers speak for, and thus characterize, themselves, see "Night, Death, Mississippi" in *Angle of Ascent*, pp. 87–88.

10. Wright's poem originally appeared in *New Masses* 11 (June 26, 1934): 16, and is reprinted in *Negro Caravan*, pp. 401–3. See also Brown's original *Southern Road* (New York: Harcourt, Brace, 1932), and his more recent *The Collected Poems of Sterling A. Brown* (New York: Harper & Row, 1982).

11. See the account of a 1974 Connecticut interview in Gendron's unpublished dissertation, pp. 68–71.

12. From a letter written by Hayden in 1970, excerpted in *Modern and Contemporary Afro-American Poetry*, ed. Bernard Bell (Boston: Allyn & Bacon, 1972), p. 175.

13. From *Conversations with Writers*, ed. Richard Layman, 1:176.

*Chapter Three*

1. See McCluskey, *How I Write*, p. 143.

2. Ibid., p. 144.

3. Ibid., p. 143.

4. See Gendron, "Robert Hayden," pp. 202–4, for Hayden's interview commentary about his foster mother's neuroses and psychosomatic suffering.

5. Gendron interview, pp. 200–201.

6. As Hayden once commented, "Life is shot through with ironies, and I think that if you have a sense of the dramatic then you have a sense of the ironical" (Gendron, "Robert Hayden," p. 166).

7. In this concealment, Hayden of course left the poem open to misinterpretations of it as a racial message about the black necessity to "wear a mask" *à la* Paul Dunbar's poem. In this regard, see Maurice J. O'Sullivan's wrong-headed article "The Mask of Allusion in Robert Hayden's 'The Diver' " in *CLA Journal* 17, no. 1 (September 1973): 85–92. For the author's intriguing comments on "The Diver," consult McCluskey, *How I Write*, p. 166.

8. McCluskey, *How I Write*, pp. 151–52.

9. Gendron, "Robert Hayden," p. 218.

10. Hayden cited a local evangelistic hustler named Prophet Jones as his prototype for "Witch Doctor," but Jones served only as "inspiration" for this unique creation (Gendron, "Robert Hayden," pp. 190–91).

11. Although Hayden explained some aspects of the poem to Dennis Gendron, that scholar avoided critical discussion of "Witch Doctor" in his dissertation on Hayden's work. Another dissertation, purportedly "A Critical Study" of Hayden's poetry by Charles H. Lynch, omits any mention of the poem. Contrarily, David Galler probably had "Witch Doctor" in mind when he accused Hayden of "hyper-erudition" in his 1967 *Poetry* review of *Selected Poems*. Hayden also mentions in the Gendron interview that "LeRoi Jones [Imamu Amiri Baraka] criticized it [the poem] 'way back there because it was full of fancy-pants words and so on" (p. 190).

*Chapter Four*

1. McCluskey, *How I Write*, p. 163.

2. Hayden discusses at some length three of his Mexico poems in *How I Write*, pp. 195–204. Subsequent quotations of his remarks are from that interview.

3. Hayden began "Middle Passage" in the late 1930s and finished an initial version in 1943; it appeared in *Phylon* in 1945 (4, no. 3, pp. 247–53). A revised version was published in *Cross Section: 1945*. Hayden again revised the poem in preparation for *A Ballad of Remembrance*.

4. Hayden describes in some detail the evolution and epic intent of "Middle Passage" during the McCluskey interview, pp. 169–76.

5. For a sustained analysis of the poem, see my article " 'Middle Passage': Robert Hayden's Anti-Epic," in *CLA Journal* 22, no. 4 (June 1979):304–18. The treatment of the poem that follows is either abstracted or quoted from that article.

6. McCluskey, *How I Write*, p. 176.

7. "Jesus Savior, Pilot Me" was originally a six-stanza poem written by Edward Hopper, who first published the poem in *The Sailors' Magazine* in 1871. Hopper then selected the first, fifth, and sixth stanzas to be set to music by John Edgar Gould, and the resultant hymn was published in the *Baptist Praise Book* in the same year and presently appears in the hymnals of several denominations.

8. "Corposant" denotes "St. Elmo's fire," a luminous electrical glow caused by corona discharge on masts of ships. Since this phenomenon was identified by sailors with St. Elmo, the patron saint of sailors, and since the term "corposant" derives from the latin *corpus sanctum* ("holy body"), quite likely Hayden uses the term to pose further ironic religious implications.

9. In the spring of 1839, Joseph Cinquez (a Spanish name assigned him in place of his African name, Singbe or Singbe-pieh) led a slave revolt aboard the *Amistad* while being transported with fifty-two other slaves from Havana to Port Principe. After the slaves killed two of their captors and gained control of the ship, they forced the two spared Spanish slavers to navigate eastward for Africa. For sixty-three days the ship zigzagged up the Atlantic coast as the Spaniards sailed east by day and reversed course by night. Finally Cinquez and the others were taken into custody near Long Island. The subsequent trial concluded with former President John Quincy Adams arguing the case before the Supreme Court, claiming that Cinquez and the surviving thirty-four Africans were neither slaves nor criminals but "self emancipated" free persons. The Africans were released and returned to Sierra Leone in 1841. Several detailed accounts of the *Amistad* incident are now in print; Hayden's chief source was the first chapter of Muriel Rukeyser's biography of *Willard Gibbs* (New York: Doubleday, Doran & Co., 1942), pp. 16–46.

10. A reproduction of this portrait appears in Rukeyser's *Willard Gibbs*, facing page 26.

11. The phrenological description, composed by a Mr. Fletcher after he had examined Cinquez, appears as a footnote in the context of "biographical sketches" compiled in John Warner Barber's *A History of*

*the Amistad Captives* (New Haven, Conn.: E. L. & J. W. Barber, 1840), pp. 9–10. Fletcher's description concludes, "In fact, such an African head is seldom to be seen, and doubtless in other circumstances would have been an honor to his race."

12. Quoted from the *New London Gazette* in Mary Cable's *Black Odyssey* (New York: Viking Press, 1971), p. 39.

13. See *William Styron's Nat Turner: Ten Black Writers Respond*, ed. John Henrik Clarke (Boston: Beacon Press, 1968).

14. See "Robert Hayden: Poet Laureate," *Negro Digest* 15 (June 1966):41–42.

15. "Frederick Douglass" initially appeared in *Atlantic Monthly*, February 1947, p. 124.

16. What follows draws rather freely upon my brief article "Robert Hayden's 'Frederick Douglass': Form and Meaning in a Modern Sonnet," *CLA Journal* 17, no. 1 (September 1973):79–84.

*Chapter Five*

1. See O'Brien, *Interviews*, p. 120. In accord with his reluctance to perform the critic's task by interpreting "The Diver," Hayden later also chose to leave speculation about "Sphinx" to the speculators. He came to regret the concrete suggestions for interpretation he afforded some interviewers when he beheld their subsequent seeming obsessions with particular lines of analysis drawn from the poet's comments, but stretched thinly into a narrow interpretive line reaching beyond or diverging from those atypically unguarded comments on his work.

2. See Gendron, "Robert Hayden," p. 168, and Charles H. Lynch, "Robert Hayden and Gwendolyn Brooks: A Critical Study," unpublished doctoral dissertation, New York University, 1977, pp. 81–82.

3. Gendron, "Robert Hayden," pp. 169–71.

4. See *The Riverside Shakespeare*, ed. G. Blakemore Evans et al. (Boston: Houghton Mifflin, 1974), p. 1762.

5. "Sailing to Byzantium," from *The Tower* (1928), reprinted in *The Selected Poems of William Butler Yeats*, ed. M. L. Rosenthal (New York: Macmillan, 1962), p. 95. Of course, Hayden's title, "Lear Is Gay," is from Yeats's poem "Lapis Lazuli" (1938); ibid., pp. 159–60.

6. O'Brien, *Interviews*, pp. 117–18.

7. For *Angle of Ascent* (1975) Hayden drastically revised "Words in the Mourning Time." At his editor's behest, to avoid delay in publication, he excised the Vietnam and racial protest poems, retaining only sections I, VI, and X, renumbered I, II, and III. Hayden, however, confided in his personal secretary, Mr. Fred Glaysher, that he planned to restore someday most of those deleted sections.

8. In these few packed lines Hayden alludes to the titles of major

works expressive of the black experience by Ralph Ellison (*Invisible Man*, 1952), Richard Wright (*Black Boy*, 1945; *Native Son*, 1940; "The Man Who Lived Underground," 1944), and James Baldwin (*Nobody Knows My Name*, 1961).

9. Malcolm X, *The Autobiography of Malcolm X*, with the assistance of Alex Haley (New York: Grove Press, 1966).

10. Hayden privately felt that given more time Malcolm X would have been led toward religious principles similar to those of the Baha'i Faith: "I believe Malcolm would have come to Baha'i or something like that, close to that." Gendron, "Robert Hayden," p. 126.

11. O'Brien, *Interviews*, p. 123.

12. Aside from textual evidence, Hayden's interest in symbolic analogy, beyond accurately describing a natural phenomenon, can be inferred from his candid acknowledgment that in fact he had never seen a night-blooming cereus in bloom when he chose the cactus plant for his metaphoric vehicle. In the same interview he contrasted his skepticism with his wife's optimism: "Erma is the positive, the affirmative one in the family. . . . As I think of our life together, she would always find a way toward a solution, toward something affirmative. . . . I tend to be a skeptical believer about everything, and Erma's not like that." Fetrow, New York interview, December 15, 1979.

*Chapter Six*

1. Alex Haley, *Roots* (New York: Doubleday, 1976).

2. Gabriel García Márquez, *Leaf Storm and Other Stories*, tr. Gregory Rabassa (New York: Harper & Row, 1972), pp. 105–12.

3. Ralph Ellison, "The Art of Fiction," *Shadow and Act* (New York: New American Library, 1966), pp. 177–78.

4. That 1942 prize-winning manuscript contained also Hayden's first poem about John Brown, called "Fire Image." Space limitations preclude an assessment of that portrait, or a comparison with its modern counterpart; indeed, analysis of Robert Hayden's revisionary habits, trends, and results could take up another full-length study.

5. For full quotation of this penultimate version of "Homage," see Michael S. Harper, "Remembering Robert Hayden," *Carleton Miscellany* 18, no. 3 (Winter 1980):231–34.

6. With the exception of the racially anonymous "Rag Man" in *American Journal* (1978, p. 15; 1982, p. 17), all seven late portrait poems depict racial heroes. For an analysis of "The Rag Man," see my essay "Robert Hayden's 'The Rag Man' and the Metaphysics of the Mundane," *Research Studies* 47, no. 3 (September 1979):188–90.

7. See "Double Feature" in *Voices: A Quarterly of Poetry* 140 (Winter 1950):23. Both "Double Feature" and "The Dogwood Trees"

appeared in the *Michigan Quarterly Review* (19, no. 1 [Winter 1980]: 92–93) prior to their inclusion in the 1982 *American Journal*.

8. This phrasing illustrates Hayden's love of, and skill in, ironical word play. With such language he emphasizes the joyous glorification of "soul" music by "sinners," who are scowled at, or "lorded" over, by righteously sullen "churchfolk."

# Selected Bibliography

PRIMARY SOURCES

(Listed Chronologically)


1. Published Works
A. Books of Poetry
*Heart-Shape in the Dust*. Detroit: Falcon Press, 1940.
*The Lion and the Archer: Poems*. With Myron O'Higgins. Nashville: Hemphill Press, 1948.
*Figure of Time: Poems*. Nashville: Hemphill Press, 1955.
*A Ballad of Remembrance*. London: Paul Breman, 1962.
*Selected Poems*. New York: October House, 1966.
*Words in the Mourning Time*. New York: October House, 1970.
*The Night-Blooming Cereus*. London: Paul Breman, 1972.
*Angle of Ascent: New and Selected Poems*. New York: Liveright, 1975.
*American Journal*. Taunton, Mass.: Effendi Press, 1978.
*American Journal*. New York: Liveright, 1982.

B. Essays and Critical Statements
"Black Writers' Views on Literary Lions and Values." *Negro Digest* 17 (January 1968):33, 84–85.
"A Letter from Robert Hayden." *Negro Digest* 17 (January 1968):98.
"Preface." *The New Negro*. Edited by Alain Locke. New York: Atheneum, 1968, pp. ix–xix. Reprint of 1925 edition.
"A Portfolio of Recent American Poems." *World Order* 5 (Spring 1971):33.
"Recent American Poetry—Portfolio II." *World Order* 9 (Summer 1975):44–45.

C. Interviews
*How I Write / 1*. With Paul McCluskey. New York: Harcourt Brace Jovanovich, 1972.
*Interviews with Black Writers*. With John O'Brien. New York: Liveright, 1973.
"Conversations with Americans." *World Order* 10 (Winter 1975–76): 46–53.

*Conversations with Writers.* With Richard Layman. Detroit: Gale Research, 1977.

D. Anthologies Edited

*Kaleidoscope: Poems by American Negro Poets.* New York: Harcourt Brace World, 1967.

*Afro-American Literature: An Introduction.* Coeditor with David J. Burrows and Frederick R. Lapides. New York: Harcourt Brace Jovanovich, 1971.

2. Unpublished Materials

A. Essays

"How It Strikes a Contemporary." Final Address delivered as Consultant in Poetry at the Library of Congress, May 8, 1978.

"From the Life: Some Remembances." Written in conjunction with filming of a documentary on Hayden's biography in 1979.

B. Phonograph Recordings

*Spectrum in Black: Poems by 20th Century Black Poets.* Scott, Foresman.

*Today's Poets: Their Poems, Their Voices.* Volume 4. Folkways Records.

*Today's Poets.* Volume 4. Scholastic Records.


SECONDARY SOURCES


1. Books

Brown, Sterling A., Davis, Arthur P., and Lee, Ulysses, eds. *The Negro Caravan.* Reprint of 1941 Dryden Press edition. New York: Arno Press, 1970. Seminal anthology of black literature; includes five of Hayden's earliest poems.

Davis, Arthur P. *From the Dark Tower: Afro-American Writers 1900 to 1960.* Washington, D.C.: Howard University Press, 1974. Includes useful synopsis of Hayden's biography and work.

Gayle, Addison, Jr. *Black Expression: Essays by and About Black Americans in the Creative Arts.* New York: Weybright & Talley, 1969. Includes a brief but insightful essay on Hayden by Arna Bontemps.

Harper, Michael S., and Stepto, Robert B., eds. *Chant of Saints: A Gathering of Afro-American Literature, Art and Scholarship.* Urbana: University of Illinois Press, 1979. Landmark volume containing writings by and about Robert Hayden among others.

Hughes, Langston, and Bontemps, Arna, eds. *The Poetry of the Negro 1746-1949*. Garden City, N.Y.: Doubleday, 1949. Contains eight of Hayden's best early poems.

Littlejohn, David. *Black on White: A Critical Survey of Writings by American Negroes*. New York: Grossman, 1966. Quotes from and praises "Middle Passage," but little else.

Major, Clarence. *The Dark and the Feeling: Black American Writers and their Work*. New York: Third Press, 1974. Notes Hayden's wide neglect by devoting a single paragraph to him.

Whitlow, Roger. *Black American Literature: A Critical History*. Chicago: Nelson Hall, 1973. Short biographical sketch, with brief introduction to, and quotation from, "Middle Passage."


2. Articles and Reviews

Davis, Charles T. "Robert Hayden's Use of History." In: *Modern Black Poets*, edited by Donald B. Gibson. Englewood Cliffs, N.J.: Prentice-Hall, 1973, pp. 96-111. Comprehensive discussion of Hayden's heritage poems.

Faulkner, Howard. " 'Transformed by Steeps of Flight': The Poetry of Robert Hayden." *CLA Journal* 21, no. 2 (December 1977):282-91. Analysis of Hayden's style to highlight recurrent theme of transformation.

Fetrow, Fred M. "Robert Hayden's 'Frederick Douglass': Form and Meaning in a Modern Sonnet." *CLA Journal* 17, no. 1 (September 1973):79-84. Examines Hayden's innovative conjunction of prosody and theme.

―――. " 'Middle Passage': Robert Hayden's Anti-Epic." *CLA Journal* 22, no. 4 (June 1979):304-18. A study of Hayden's ironic use of epic structure and conventions for thematic purpose.

―――. "Robert Hayden's 'The Rag Man' and the Metaphysics of the Mundane." *Research Studies* 47, no. 3 (September 1979):188-90. Psychoanalytic approach to character portrait.

Galler, David. "Three Recent Volumes," *Poetry* 110 (July 1967):267-69. Review of *Selected Poems*.

Harper, Michael S. "Remembering Robert E. Hayden." *Carleton Miscellany* 18, no. 3 (Winter 1980):231-34. Rich embroidery on Hayden's life and work.

―――, ed. Special memorial issue of *Obsidian* dedicated to Robert Hayden (forthcoming, 1984).

Lester, Julius. "For a world where a man is a man, a poet a poet." *New York Times Book Review*, January 24, 1971, pp. 4-5, 22. Review of *Words in the Mourning Time*.

Lewis, Richard O. "A Literary-Psychoanalytic Interpretation of Robert

Hayden's 'Market.' " *Black American Literature Forum* 9
(1975):21–24. An example of excesses and limitations of
psychological criticism; almost interesting.

**Novak, Michael Paul.** "Meditative, Ironic, Richly Human: The Poetry
of Robert Hayden." *Midwest Quarterly* 15, no. 3 (Spring
1974):276–85. Brief reviewlike sampler of Hayden's best-known
poems as an introduction to a neglected poet.

**O'Sullivan, Maurice J., Jr.** "The Mask of Allusion in Robert Hayden's
'The Diver.' " *CLA Journal* 17, no. 1 (September 1973):85–92.
Provocative but faulty interpretation of an allegorical poem.

**Pool, Rosey E.** "Robert Hayden: Poet Laureate." *Negro Digest* 15
(June 1966): 39–43. "An Assessment" and an appreciation of
Hayden as the winner of "the prize for anglophone poetry at the
First World Festival of Negro Arts."

**Post, Constance J.** "Image and Idea in the Poetry of Robert Hayden."
*CLA Journal* 20, no. 2 (December 1976):164–75. Reductive view
of Hayden's work in limited terms of a central image and primary
theme.

**Turco, Lewis.** "Angle of Ascent: The Poetry of Robert Hayden."
*Michigan Quarterly Review* 16, no. 2 (Spring 1977):199–219.
Methodically and convincingly defends Hayden as an artist who
transcends, yet is true to, his black heritage.

**Williams, Wilburn, Jr.** "Covenant of Timelessness and Time: Symbolism and History in Robert Hayden's *Angle of Ascent.*" *The
Massachusetts Review* 18, no. 4 (Winter 1977): 731–49. Comprehensive study that relates Hayden's symbolic mode and his fascination with history, both personal and public.


3. Poems about Robert Hayden

**Harper, Michael S.** "Bird of Paradise." *Carleton Miscellany* 18, no. 3
(Winter 1980):235.

———. "Mr. Hayden Falls into Place." *Works in Progress* 10 (1980):
77–78. Brown University.


4. Doctoral dissertations on Robert Hayden

**Gendron, Dennis J.** "Robert Hayden: A View of His Life and Development as a Poet." University of North Carolina, Chapel Hill, 1975.

**Lynch, Charles H.** "Robert Hayden and Gwendolyn Brooks: A Critical
Study." New York University, 1977.

**Williams, Pontheolla Taylor.** "A Critical Analysis of the Poetry of
Robert Hayden through His Middle Years." Yale University,
1980.

# Index